HIGHER MODERN STUDIES

Social Issues in the UK:
Wealth & Health Inequalities

Tracey James

HODDER
GIBSON
PART OF HACHETTE LIVRE UK

The Publishers would like to thank the following for permission to reproduce copyright material:

Photo credits
Page 2 (left) © Matt Cardy/Alamy, (right) © 67photo/Alamy; page 3 © Dan Atkin/Alamy; page 6 © Hodder Gibson; page 7 © Troy Aossey/Taxi/Getty Images; page 13 © Child Poverty Action Group; page 14 © David White/Alamy; page 20 © Tom Kidd/Alamy; page 24 © PA Photos; page 25 (left) © LANDOV/PA Photos (right) © fStop/Alamy; page 37 © Helen King/CORBIS; page 46 © Bernd Opitz/Taxi/Getty Images; page 50 (top) © plainpicture GmbH & Co. KG/Alamy, (bottom) © Picture Partners/Alamy; page 52 © Noel Hendrickson/Digital Vision/Getty Images; page 53 (top) © Jon Arnold Images Ltd/Alamy, (bottom) © South West Images Scotland/Alamy; page 55 © Andrew Fox/Alamy; page 57 © Keystone/Getty Images; page 59 © Alex Segre/Alamy; page 60 (left) © 67photo/Alamy, (right) © Christopher Furlong/Getty Images; page 65 © Scott Barbour/Getty Images; page 66 © Scottish Government; page 67 © PA Photos; page 69 © Duncan Hale-Sutton/Alamy; page 70 (top) © PA Photos, (bottom) © NHS 24; page 72 © Hodder Gibson; page 74 © The Photolibrary Wales/Alamy; page 75 © Hodder Gibson; page 76 © Sally and Richard Greenhill/Alamy; page 78 (left) © Ingram, (right) Stockbyte/Getty Images; page 79 © www.purestockX.com; page 80 (left) © Peter Lawson/Rex Features, (right) © Alex Segre/Alamy.

Index © Indexing Specialists (UK) Ltd.

Every effort has been made to trace all copyright holders, but if any have been inadvertently overlooked the Publishers will be pleased to make the necessary arrangements at the first opportunity.

Although every effort has been made to ensure that website addresses are correct at time of going to press, Hodder Gibson cannot be held responsible for the content of any website mentioned in this book. It is sometimes possible to find a relocated web page by typing in the address of the home page for a website in the URL window of your browser.

Hachette's policy is to use papers that are natural, renewable and recyclable products and made from wood grown in sustainable forests. The logging and manufacturing processes are expected to conform to the environmental regulations of the country of origin.

Orders: please contact Bookpoint Ltd, 130 Milton Park, Abingdon, Oxon OX14 4SB. Telephone: (44) 01235 827720. Fax: (44) 01235 400454. Lines are open 9.00 – 5.00, Monday to Saturday, with a 24-hour message answering service. Visit our website at www.hoddereducation.co.uk. Hodder Gibson can be contacted direct on: Tel: 0141 848 1609; Fax: 0141 889 6315; email: hoddergibson@hodder.co.uk

© Tracey James 2008
First published in 2008 by
Hodder Gibson, an imprint of Hodder Education,
Part of Hachette Livre UK,
2a Christie Street
Paisley PA1 1NB

Impression number   5 4 3 2 1
Year   2012 2011 2010 2009 2008

Cover photos © Edifice Photo Library (top) and © Chris James/Epicscotland (bottom)
Illustrations by Jeff Edwards
Typeset in Minion Pro 12/15pt by Fakenham Photosetting, Fakenham, Norfolk
Printed in Italy

A catalogue record for this title is available from the British Library

ISBN-13: 978 0340 965 191

Contents

What this book does   v

Introduction

Living in Britain   1
The Welfare State   2

1   Inequalities in income, wealth and living standards

Evidence   6
Reasons   19
Employment and Unemployment   21
Responses   24
Social Security (DWP) Benefits   26
Welfare Reform and Recent Government Initiatives   30
Social Class   35

2   Gender inequality

Background   40
Evidence   42
Reasons   45
Responses   48

3   Inequality and ethnicity

Background   54
Evidence   62
Reasons   64
Responses   65

4 Inequalities in health

The National Health Service (NHS)   68
Evidence   72
Reasons   76
Responses   78

5 The SQA exam

Paper 1   82
Quick Revision Test Questions   86
Paper 2   87

Index

Index   91

What this book does

This book is designed to help you pass Study Theme 2: Inequalities in Wealth and Health in the UK. This topic covers half (45 out of the total 90) of the marks available in Higher Modern Studies. It is a wide-ranging topic. The way to organise your study is to always think of three aspects of inequalities:

1 **Evidence** of inequalities from reports, studies, documentaries etc.
2 **Reasons** for inequalities such as ill health, poverty and lifestyle.
3 **Responses** to inequalities by central government, local authorities, charities and pressure groups (NGOs) and individuals.

You need to be able to discuss these three headings with reference to:

- income and wealth
- ethnicity and gender
- health.

You need to be familiar with the **principles of the Welfare State** and the collectivist or individualist debate over welfare provision.

 Throughout this book, this icon indicates a 15 mark exam-type question. There are also some suggested outlines and sample answers. These have been provided to give you some guidance on what an answer could include but are not meant to constitute checklists or templates. There are always many possible ideas to discuss that would also receive credit.

Introduction

Living in Britain

Britain is a wealthy country. However, there are important differences within British society in living standards. British people expect a reasonable standard of living. They have also come to expect that the government and/or local council and other agencies provide services such as health and social security. Recent years have seen these ideas challenged as some politicians have questioned whether the Welfare State set up in the 1945–51 era is still appropriate to the twenty-first century.

> **1** What do British people now expect from the government and other agencies?

In July 2007 the population was just over 60 million. The population has increased by over 2 million since 1980. It is forecast to rise to a peak of around 60 million in 2020. The population is likely to start falling from about 2025, owing to fewer births and an increase in the number of deaths in the elderly population. In Scotland, in July 2006, the population was just over 5 million.

At birth the expectation of life for a man in Britain is now 77 years and for a woman it is 81 years, compared with 45 years for men and 49 years for women in 1901. Among the elderly, the number aged over 85 has more than doubled since 1971 and is now over 1 million. This means that, like other developed countries, the UK has a population with a growing percentage of old people, who pay little or no tax but often require care. More young people stay on at school beyond 16 and many go on to college or university. The percentage of adults of working age who pay tax and National Insurance needed to pay for public services is lower than it used to be.

The average number of persons per household in UK is now 2.3. The average household size has declined due to the growth in the numbers of the elderly who live alone or as couples, and in single parent families, and the preference for smaller families. Other features of modern family life are a big increase in cohabitation, fewer marriages and higher levels of divorce. All these put more pressure on the Welfare State.

1 What is happening to the population of Britain?

2 Explain why the population is changing. What is expected to happen to population in the future?

3 What is happening to the number of young people who stay in education after 16?

4 What has happened to the percentage of adults of working age?

5 Why is this a problem?

6 Explain why average household size has decreased.

7 Why does the Welfare State feel the pressure as the modern British family changes?

The Welfare State

When World War II ended in 1945, the Labour Government set up a Welfare State based on the Beveridge Report which was published in 1942. This aimed to provide a safety net for any British citizen who needed help at any point in their lifetime – 'from the cradle to the grave'. Beveridge named five giant evils in society as Want, Disease, Squalor, Ignorance and Illness. To deal with these Beveridge wanted:

● education for all
● affordable good quality housing

● a national health service
● a social security safety net
● full employment.

Beveridge argued that this system would provide a minimum standard of living 'below which no one should be allowed to fall'.

The Social Security system was designed as part of the Welfare State to ensure a minimum standard of living for every citizen. However, it was expected that National Insurance would cover the cost of most benefits and a relatively small amount would be needed from tax to pay for non-contributory benefits. Everyone thought that unemployment would stay at a low level and that only a small number of citizens would need help at any one time. No one realised that the Welfare State would prove so expensive.

1 Explain the phrase 'social safety net' in relation to the Welfare State.
2 Arrange the five giant evils in society alongside what Beveridge wanted from the Welfare State to tackle them to create a table.
3 What is meant by the phrase 'from the cradle to the grave'?
4 How was the Welfare State to be paid for?

The post-war Welfare State has had many successes. The National Health Service (NHS) is one of the most popular institutions in the UK. There have been advances in medical treatment; one reason why British citizens now live longer and more healthy lives. Illness is no longer inevitably followed by poverty. A range of benefits exist to help those in society who are unable to earn enough to live on. Services exist to help the unemployed back into work. Education is available free of charge at both primary and secondary levels. Further education is open to all. Housing standards have improved.

However, the aims of the Beveridge era have not been fully realised. Every year the costs of the Welfare State have risen. As the NHS provides new treatments more staff and resources are needed. Prescription charges were introduced into the NHS within a few years of its creation. Not all drugs are available to all patients. The growing number of old people need on average twice as much care as younger people yet most no longer work so do not contribute to the cost of providing care. Housing costs have risen and there is a shortage of affordable homes.

Providing for an increased elderly population is the largest single cost for the Welfare State. However, there are other groups in society who also need help from the state. Families with children, especially single parent families, are the group most affected by poverty. There are growing numbers of people with a disability, including various forms of mental illness. At times unemployment has been much larger than expected by Beveridge.

1   List the groups who are the biggest users of the Welfare State.

2   Describe the challenges facing the Welfare State today.

3   In what ways can the government meet these challenges?

It is often said that the Welfare State was based on collectivist principles. The collectivist approach means that society is responsible for all its citizens. The state (the government, local authorities etc.) has a duty to provide services such as health and education for all. Even when an individual seems to be responsible for their situation, for example, by smoking or eating a poor diet, collectivists argue that this is caused by poor life chances.

Individualists argue that it is simply down to each person to look after their health and welfare and that of their family. They argue that when the state provides for them some people give up on their responsibilities. They also argue that incentives are needed to encourage citizens to live healthy and sensible lives. They say collectivism leads to an expensive, inefficient 'nanny' state. Many individualists prefer private providers of health, education and insurance. They argue that competition between service providers keep costs down and improves efficiency.

Most people in the UK, and all the major political parties, believe in a mix of collectivism and individualism. However, the balance between what the state should do and what should be left to the individual varies. Traditionally, the Labour Party was more collectivist than the Conservatives. However, this has changed in recent years and it is now much harder to identify clear cut differences in ideology over welfare provision between the main political parties.

Even in the 1945–51 era when the Beveridge proposals were put into practice the Welfare State was a mix of collectivism and individualism. Some benefits and services were universal and available to all whether they had paid National Insurance or not. However, some benefits were means tested; only available to those who could prove their incomes were below a certain figure.

The continued existence of inequalities in the UK and the growing cost of health and welfare mean that welfare reform and the debate between collectivists and individualists are still important.

1   Draw a table to display the collectivist and individualist approaches side by side.

2   What is meant by the phrase a 'nanny state'? Can you think of any examples?

3   Write a paragraph discussing why some citizens may view the UK as a 'nanny state'.

4   Explain means tested benefits.

5   Where do the main political parties position themselves on the topics of collectivism and individualism?

6   Do you consider yourself to be a collectivist or an individualist? Give a reason for your decision.

Essay question

Your first 15 mark exam-type question! Use the framework and the information on pages 2–5 to answer the question. Also read over the section on the SQA exam Paper One in Chapter 5. The essay outline below is provided to give you some guidance on what an answer could include. It is not meant as a checklist as there are many possible ideas to discuss that would also receive credit.

1   To what extent has the Welfare State achieved its original aims.

Essay outline:

- **Introduction** – reference to post-war Britain, five areas it was concerned with, social safety net, 'cradle to the grave' etc.
- **Paragraph 1** – partly successful – major problem has been handling ever increasing costs.
  Raising taxes is not an attractive option for political parties. What groups need help?
- **Paragraph 2** – NHS – ever increasing costs, increase in life expectancy, new drugs and treatments – however, treatments sometimes rationalised leading to inequalities
- **Paragraph 3** – social security is the most expensive government expenditure, more targeted, means tested Department for Work and Pensions (DWP) benefits required, individual responsibility emphasised by political parties.
- **Paragraph 4** – council houses have been sold off, lack of affordable housing in many areas. State school still popular and many are successful. Many go on to further education/higher education thanks to student loans systems. Some turn to private healthcare instead of NHS. Collectivism/individualism.
- **In conclusion** – citizens live longer thanks to the Welfare State. Need for welfare reform?

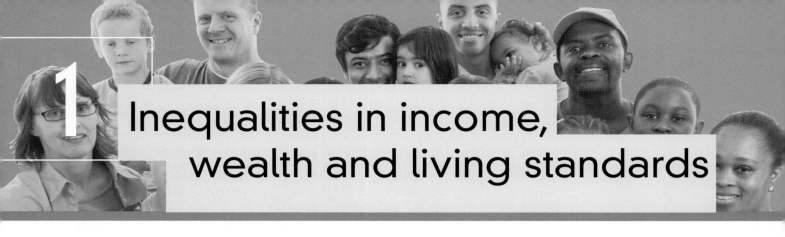

Inequalities in income, wealth and living standards

Evidence

It is important to be aware of the difference between wealth and income. Wealth comes from owning items such as property, investments and possessions such as jewellery. Wealth has to be turned into some form of cash before it can be spent. Income is money that is available to spend. Most income comes from wages or salaries but income can also come from rent, profits gained from selling shares as well as money from social security benefits and pensions.

Figure 1.1 →

The UK is a wealthy country. A country's wealth can be measured by its gross domestic product (GDP) which adds the value of all goods and services produced each year. Gross National Product (GNP) is GDP plus the value of trade with other countries and investments made abroad by British citizens and companies. However, to compare living standards for individuals it is necessary to calculate GDP per person. The UK economy is currently the world's fifth largest behind the USA, Japan, Germany and China.

Wages and salaries remain the main source of income for most people of working age. Average incomes have increased in the UK. However, there are differences in income and these differences have increased in recent years. Taxes now take a lower proportion of personal income than in many other European countries. Politicians know that increases in tax, especially Income Tax, are unpopular with voters. Benefits are an important source of income for many British families. Some rely on benefits entirely while others use benefits to 'top up' their income to an acceptable level.

For older people pensions are the main source of income. Most elderly people rely on pensions and savings. The age at which people retire now varies more between individuals due to an increase in early retirement. Someone who only has the basic state retirement pension will have to claim means tested benefits to help with the cost of essentials such as heating and rent. A growing number of elderly people have occupational pensions.

Figure 1.2 →

1 What do most people rely on as their main source of income?
2 What has happened to incomes in recent years?
3 Why are governments under pressure to keep tax down?
4 Explain why older people's incomes are different from other age groups.
5 Discuss the reasons why some old people are better off than others?

Living standards have increased in Britain. Most households now own more consumer goods, have more money to spend and are more likely to own their home. 68% of families in the UK own their own homes while 12% rent their home from the local council. Most households now own digital TV, a mobile phone, electrical appliances such as dishwashers and microwaves as well as having central heating (around 95%). The number of home computers and the use of the internet have both risen dramatically in recent years. Other evidence of increasing living standards comes in changes in eating habits. More people now eat out in restaurants while take away food shops have become common throughout the country. There has been an increase in sales of convenience foods and ready meals which are easier to prepare but more expensive than cooking from basic ingredients. Most households have a car and many have two. There has been a dramatic increase in the number of British people who take foreign holidays with the rise of the low budget airlines which serve most British cities.

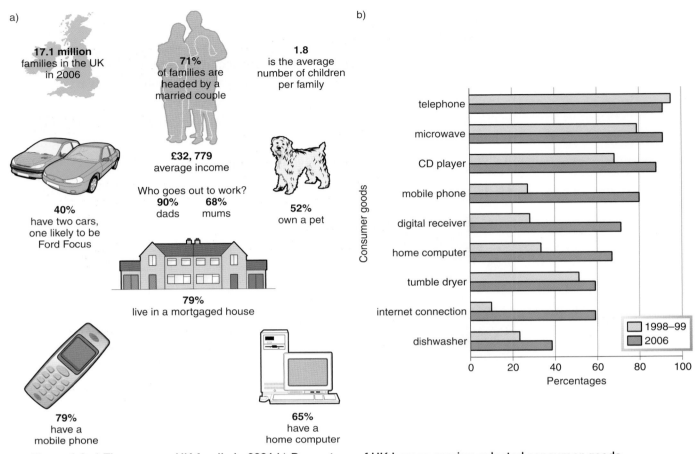

a)

17.1 million
families in the UK
in 2006

71%
of families are
headed by a
married couple

1.8
is the average
number of children
per family

£32, 779
average income

Who goes out to work?
90% **68%**
dads mums

40%
have two cars,
one likely to be
Ford Focus

52%
own a pet

79%
live in a mortgaged house

79%
have a
mobile phone

65%
have a
home computer

b)

Consumer goods: telephone, microwave, CD player, mobile phone, digital receiver, home computer, tumble dryer, internet connection, dishwasher

Percentages 0 20 40 60 80 100

Legend: 1998–99, 2006

Figure 1.3 a) The average UK family in 2006 b) Percentage of UK homes owning selected consumer goods (1998-99, 2006)

Source: http://news.bbc.co.uk/1/hi/uk/7071611.stm

Families with children usually have less to spend per person than couples or single adults. In 2006, the average family income was £32,779 before tax. According to Office of National Statistics (ONS) figures, an average family – made up of 3.9 people – spends £601.20 a week, compared with a couple's average spend of £527.30. In other words, the household spends £155.60 per person compared with a couple's spend of £263.60 per person.

1 Use the figures and the information on pages 6–8 to write a paragraph describing a typical UK family. Remember not to simply list lots of figures but try and comment on trends.

Figure 1.4 on the next page compares the poorest and richest households by the amount of consumer goods they own. The poorest households in Britain are not that poor compared with other countries in the world. Half of the poorest households in the UK own a mobile phone and also have digital or cable TV, while one-third have a computer in the home and a fifth have internet access.

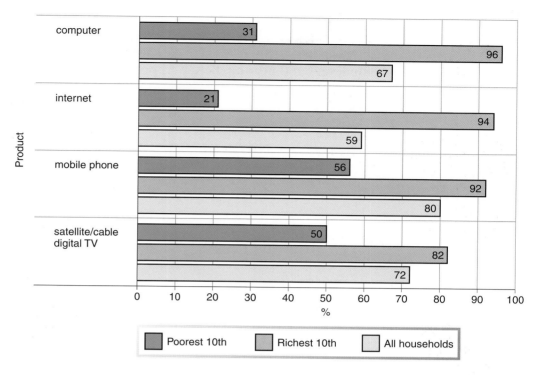

Figure 1.4 Goods owned by household income groups in the UK (2006) →

1 Using the figures on pages 8–9, explain what has happened to the living standards of most British people? What evidence can you give to support this statement?

Personal wealth is often misunderstood. It means the value of your assets not just the money you have to spend. For most people their main asset is their house. In the UK, around two-thirds of households now own their own homes and fewer people now rent their homes so 'wealth' has increased. In practice home owners cannot use their 'wealth' as they need a house to live in. If they sell one home they have to buy another.

Wealth is less evenly distributed than income. The richest 10% of the population have half of the wealth. The proportion of wealth held in stocks, shares and unit trusts nearly doubled between 1981 and 1995, to 15%. Many schemes encourage workers to buy or receive shares in the company they work for.

1 What does wealth actually mean?
2 Why have some people had increases in their wealth?

Obviously better off people have more money to spend. However, the percentage of a person's income that they spend on different things varies. Poor people spend a larger proportion of their income on essentials such as food, rent and heating. Better off people spend a higher proportion on transport, clothing and entertainment. Poorer people are more likely to spend money on cigarettes.

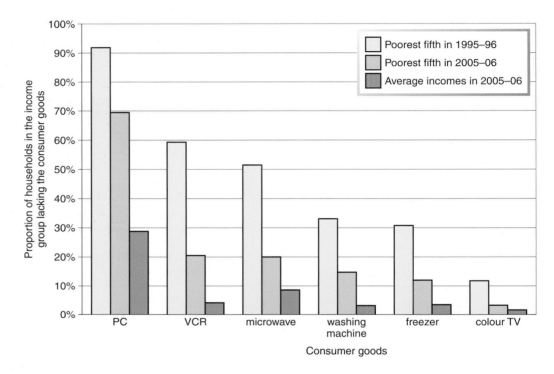

**Figure 1.5
Proportion of UK
households lacking
consumer goods
(1995-96 and
2005-6)** →

Source: Institute for Social and Economic Research UK

1 Discuss differences in the way rich and poor people spend their incomes.

2 Explain these differences and give reasons why they exist.

There are also regional differences in living standards. Traditionally South East England has had the highest living standards. The fact that incomes have, on average, been lower in Scotland and Northern England led to the concept of a North–South Divide within the United Kingdom. This was linked to economic problems in remote regions as well as the decline of traditional industries such as mining, shipbuilding and engineering in Northern England, Wales and Scotland. This is illustrated in Table 1.

However, the North–South Divide oversimplifies the true situation. There are greater differences within Scotland than between Scotland and South East England. Edinburgh and Aberdeen usually have lower levels of unemployment and poverty than Glasgow and Dundee. Even within cities there are striking

Comparisons between the rich and the poor

In wealthier areas the following occur more than average:	In poorer areas the following occur more than average:
Detached, larger houses	Flats, council houses
More than one car	Public transport
Higher educational qualifications	School leaver
Self employed	Weekly wage or benefits
More people working as senior managers or professionals	Manual/unskilled/semi skilled jobs
More likely to have people of Chinese or Indian origin living nearby	More likely to have people of Pakistani or Bangladeshi origin in the street
Timeshare holidays	Camping holidays
Going to coffee bars	Going to night clubs
Joining sailing clubs	Joining bowling/angling clubs
Bridge	Bingo
Reading the Radio Times	Reading the TV Times
Listening to BBC Radio	Listening to Commercial Radio
iPods	Games consoles
Online banking	Online games
Drinking alcohol at home	Smoking tobacco
Eating at restaurants	Eating from takeaways
Private healthcare	NHS
Private school	State school

Source: http://www.caci.co.uk/pdfs/won2006abridged.pdf

differences in living standards and life expectancy between prosperous suburbs and some council housing estates.

There are regional differences in the way money is spent. Transport and heating costs more in Scotland due to remoteness and the climate. Scots and people from the North of England spend more on smoking than people in Southern England.

Costs of smoking

A smoking habit of 20 cigarettes per day costs between £1,600 and £1,800 per year. Poorer smokers spend a disproportionately large share of their income on cigarettes compared with more affluent smokers. Among the most deprived groups – including lone parents in receipt of state benefits – three out of four families smoke and spend a seventh of their disposable income on cigarettes.

Source: http://newash.org.uk/files/documents/ASH_98.pdf (ASH website)

Table 1 Regional difference in employment and unemployment 2006

Region	Employment rate (percentage)	Unemployment (%)
UK Average	74.5	5.6
England	74.7	5.7
Scotland	75.2	5.0
Wales	72.1	5.4
Northern Ireland	68.9	4.7
North East	70.9	6.9
North West	73.5	5.6
Yorkshire and Humberside	73.5	6.0
East Midlands	77.1	5.3
West Midlands	73.9	6.1
East of England	77.0	5.0
London	69.5	8.0
South East	78.9	4.5
South West	77.8	3.9

Source: Labour Market Statistics, November 2006, ONS.

Children from less advantaged social backgrounds are more likely to start smoking than children from more affluent backgrounds. However, by their 30s, half of the better off young people have stopped smoking while three-quarters of those in the lowest income group carry on.

The impact of the recent smoking bans in Scotland and England is difficult to assess. The new regulation was set up to reduce the number of deaths from second-hand smoke. Some reports indicate a fall in the sales of cigarettes in England. It is difficult to predict if this is a trend for the future but many hope that the smoking ban combined with a rise in the age to purchase cigarettes to 18 will have a positive effect on the health of the nation.

What is poverty?

Individuals, families and groups in the population can be said to be in poverty when they lack the resources to have the living conditions and amenities which are customary in our society. Poorer people are dependent on the DWP benefits for all or a large part of their income.

1 Write a definition for poverty.

2 What do many poor people rely on for income?

How poverty is measured

Some groups are more affected than other groups by poverty. Poverty in Britain is relative rather than absolute. However, if you are on a low income in this country you compare yourself with better off British people not those in absolute poverty in other parts of the world. The official definition of poverty used by the DWP class the poverty line at 60% of median household income (Households Below Average Income, HBAI). Data are often presented before and after housing costs have been accounted for; the government prefers before housing costs, because similar international data exists to allow comparison. Pressure groups like the Child Poverty Action Group (CPAG) prefer to use data after housing costs. They argue that this gives a better indication of household's disposable income. Another measure is to say that anyone able to claim for means tested benefits such as Income Support is in poverty.

CHILD POVERTY ACTION GROUP

Figure 1.6 ➡

1 Explain the difference between relative and absolute poverty.

2 What is meant by disposable income?

The Poverty Line

In 2005/06, the DWP's poverty line – the amount of money below which, after adjusting for size and makeup of the household and after housing costs, a family was officially poor – was:

- £222 per week (£11,544 per year) for a lone parent with two children (5 and 14)
- £300 per week (£15,600 per year) for a couple with two children (5 and 14).

Figure 1.7 →

The Poverty and Social Exclusion Survey (PSE) measures poverty by identifying people who do not have a range of items considered essential for modern life, for example furniture, heating, decent clothes and somewhere to stay. This survey found that one-third of the population could be described as poor or at risk of falling into poverty.

The Scottish Index of Multiple Deprivation divides Scotland into areas and uses data on health, income, employment and education to rank them from the least to the most deprived.

Independent researchers also study poverty sometimes on behalf of charities and pressure groups. The Joseph Rowntree Foundation is the UK's largest independent social research and development charity. It supported the PSE Survey of Britain in 1999.

Who lives in poverty? (CPAG's Poverty the Facts booklet)

Poverty is greatest among families with children. Single parent families are twice as likely to be in poverty as families with two adults. In 2004, the Families and Children Study found that 8% of single parent families and 2% of couple families could not afford to eat vegetables most days. The same numbers were also found for fruit and cakes/biscuits most days. 21% of single parent families and 6% of couple families reported that they could not afford new clothes when these were needed.

On average women have lower incomes than men. Women who are single parents or who have given up careers to act as carers are more likely to be in poverty.

Although the elderly are often thought of as a poor group some retired people have comfortable incomes. The rise in house prices has had a big effect on the wealth of older people some of whom have houses now worth several hundred thousand pounds.

Any adult who is unable to work or is in poorly paid, temporary, seasonal or part-time employment is likely to have a low enough income to qualify for means tested benefits.

Several ethnic minority groups have relatively low average incomes. However, there is evidence of some improvement in women's incomes and career prospects while some ethnic minorities have similar incomes to the white majority.

Differences within groups are important but not shown by the average figures.

The extent of poverty in the UK today (CPAG)

In 2005/06, 12.7 million people in the UK (22%) were officially poor, living in households with below 60% of the median income after housing costs. Although in recent years this has been falling, in 2005/06 it rose. In 1979, 15% were in this position.

There are nearly 1 million people, or 20% of the Scottish population, living in poverty.

Unemployment – 75% of people in households where the adults are unemployed are poor. When all adults in a household are in full-time work, only 5% are poor.

Families and Household – 49% of people in single parent households are poor, compared with 24% of single people without children. 22% of people in couple households with children are poor, compared with 11% where there are no children. 16% of couple pensioners are poor. Of those pensioners who are single, 16% of men and 20% of women are poor.

Ethnicity – 20% of White people are poor, compared with 63% of Pakistani and Bangladeshi people, and 41% of Black people.

Source: Scottish Households below Average Income 2005/06

1 Summarise the information in the two shaded boxes on the extent of poverty in Scotland and the UK.

2 Write a paragraph discussing the problems of child poverty in the UK and Scotland.

3 What are the consequences of child poverty?

Child Poverty in the UK: Nations and Regions

Child Poverty rates vary widely across the UK. Although poverty is often said to be worse in the north the area with the highest concentration of child

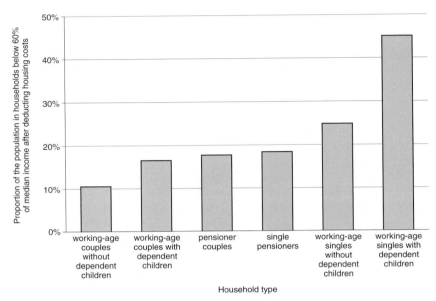

Figure 1.8 Proportion of UK population with below 60% median income in 2007 →

Source: http://www.poverty.org.uk/S03a/index.shtml

> **1** What conclusions can be made to summarise the information in Figure 1.11 on page 18?

poverty after housing costs is Inner London where over half (51%) of all children are poor. This shows that pockets of deprivation exist even in the generally prosperous south east of England.

The total number of single parent families who are very poor is small. This may seem surprising but is due to the fact that there are many more couples with or without children than those who are single parent families. The proportion of single parent families in poverty is higher than any other group. Although the elderly are often thought of as a poor group, living standards vary greatly among old people.

Child Poverty by Constituency

Within Scotland the worst concentrations of deprivation are in Glasgow where around half of the city is classed in the most deprived category. Other concentrations of poverty and deprivation are in areas around Glasgow such as Inverclyde, West Dunbartonshire and North Lanarkshire. Away from West Central Scotland, Dundee has high levels of deprivation. Although all areas have some pockets of poverty, around half of low income households in Scotland live in or around Glasgow, Dundee or Edinburgh.

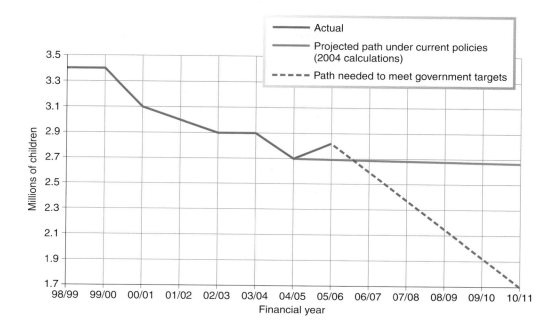

Figure 1.9 Number of children living in households with below 60% median income, actual and projected (1998–2011) ➔

Source: http://news.bbc.co.uk/1/hi/uk_politics/7066838.stm

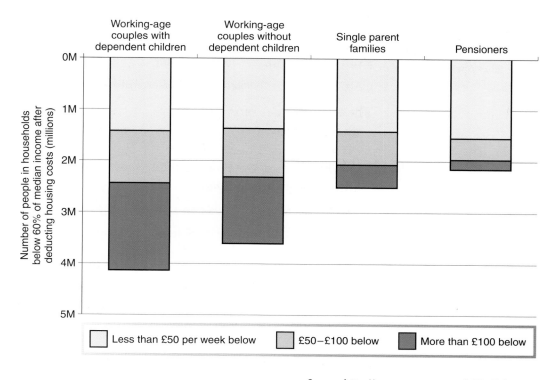

Figure 1.10 Number of people living in households with below 60% median income ➔

Source: http://www.poverty.org.uk/03a/b.jpg

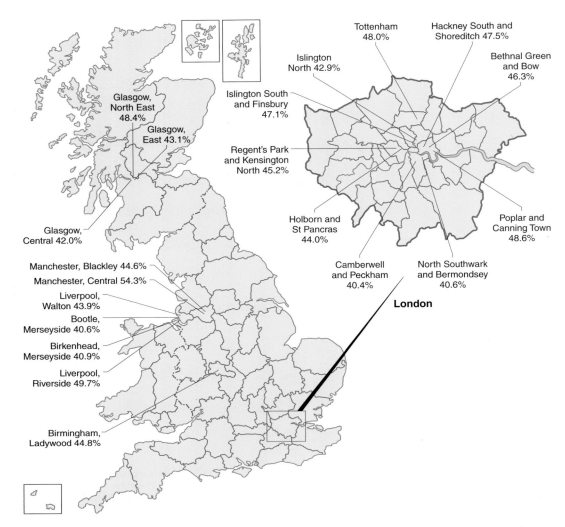

Figure 1.11 Percentage of children in families on out of work benefits in the top 20 constituencies of England, Scotland and Wales (UK average 21%) April 2005 →

Tottenham 48.0%

Hackney South and Shoreditch 47.5%

Bethnal Green and Bow 46.3%

Islington North 42.9%

Islington South and Finsbury 47.1%

Regent's Park and Kensington North 45.2%

Poplar and Canning Town 48.6%

Holborn and St Pancras 44.0%

Camberwell and Peckham 40.4%

North Southwark and Bermondsey 40.6%

London

Glasgow, North East 48.4%

Glasgow, East 43.1%

Glasgow, Central 42.0%

Manchester, Blackley 44.6%

Manchester, Central 54.3%

Liverpool, Walton 43.9%

Bootle, Merseyside 40.6%

Birkenhead, Merseyside 40.9%

Liverpool, Riverside 49.7%

Birmingham, Ladywood 44.8%

Source: http://www.jrf.org.uk/child-poverty/documents/constituency-averages.xls

1 What areas of the UK have the highest levels of child poverty? Give evidence to support your answer.

2 How do Scottish cities compare with their English counterparts?

3 Write a paragraph to explain the variation in child poverty around the UK.

Reasons

The primary cause of poverty is inadequate income, caused by unemployment or inadequate wages and benefits. Overall employment is now high at over 70% and unemployment relatively low. The risk of not being in work varies between groups and is higher for those with low skills, from certain minority ethnic groups (especially Pakistani and Bangladeshi people), and for those living in low employment areas. Other barriers to work include caring responsibilities and discrimination.

However, a job is not a guarantee of being free of poverty. Low wages, part-time work and not having two adults in work in a household all increase the risk of poverty. In 2005/06, 57% of poor children were in households where one or more parent was in work. Safety net benefits and tax credits are also often inadequate to protect families with children from poverty, and their value often remains below the poverty line.

Some DWP benefits have not been increased in line with the cost of living.

The fear of unemployment means more people will now take any job, however poorly paid. Low pay is widespread in areas such as shop work, catering, hotels and home working and often only pays the National Minimum Wage.

The increasing numbers of old people include some who only have the basic state pension. Many elderly people are too proud or do not understand how to claim means tested benefits such as Income Support.

The shortage of council houses has led more British people to buy their own home. However, this also led to record levels of repossessions of homes when the mortgage payments were not kept up.

More family break ups means financial problems especially where a mother is bringing up children unsupported. There is also the rise in the number of single parents most of whom are women. Both are linked to the cost and availability of child care.

Community Care policies have removed many mental patients and elderly people from hospitals. Some have not been able to cope on their own.

1 Make a summary of the causes of poverty.

2 In what ways can the government try and meet the needs of citizens living in poverty?

3 Do you think the government's current efforts are working? Why or why not?

Living in poverty in modern Scotland

Poverty rates among working-age adults without dependent children have risen from around 15% in the mid-1990s to 18%, despite a fall in unemployment. Unlike children, the poverty risks for working-age adults in both working and workless households are higher than a decade ago.

Figure 1.12 →

Relative to earnings, out-of-work benefits for working-age adults without children are now worth 20% less than in 1997. Two-thirds of low-paid employees are women, as many more women than men work part-time, and part-time work carries a high risk of low pay.

Source: *Monitoring poverty and social exclusion in Scotland 2006*

There are several other areas to consider. Ill health can lead to differences in life expectancy. Comparing the poorest and richest areas of Glasgow can be up 25 years for men and 15 years for women. Nearly 20% of young people leave secondary school without any Highers. This increases the probability of living in poverty later in life. Living in damp housing conditions is another problem area. 360,000 homes in Scotland are affected by dampness. The majority of Scottish council housing is below the Scottish Quality Housing Standard. 125,000 children live in overcrowded and often damp conditions which can lead to medical problems such as asthma later on in life.

Fuel Poverty is a problem for people on low income and in particular the elderly. Fuel poor households do not have enough money to properly heat their homes; this has been made worse with recent increases in fuel costs. Senior citizens are more likely to develop cold-related illnesses, such as hypothermia, in the winter months which too often results in death.

Source: http://www.povertyalliance.org/html/information/statistics.htm

1 Make brief notes on the groups of people in Scotland who live in poverty today.

2 What challenges does this lead to for central and local governments?

3 'Poverty still exists in the UK for a variety of reasons. Relative poverty has even increased.' Discuss.

4 'Despite increasing living standards inequalities in UK society have increased'. Discuss.

What are the effects of poverty on children?

On average, poverty makes people's lives shorter and less pleasant than they need be. Being on a low income leads to less choice, poor health, education and housing, basic self-esteem and the ability to participate in social activities. It also hurts society, and by affecting educational attainment it reduces the skills available to employers and damages economic growth.

- **Educational attainment** – In England in 2006, 60% of children not entitled to free school meals obtained five or more GCSEs at grades A–C, around double the 32% of children who were entitled to free school meals.
- **Health** – Poverty is associated with a higher risk of both illness and early death. Life expectancy for people in social class V (manual workers) is 7 years shorter on average than that for those in social class I (people working as managers). Children in social class V are five times more likely to die in an accident and 15 times more likely to die in a fire than children in social class I.
- **Participation** – A recent *Households Below Average Income* (HBAI) survey asked parents about their children's activities. The report found that 7% of children do not have access to leisure equipment (such as a bike), 6% do not have a hobby (karate or dancing), 11% cannot go swimming, 8% do not have friends over for tea and 6% cannot go on a school trip. The main reason for children missing out was because their parents could not afford it.

1 Discuss the ways in which poverty can affect the lives of children.

Employment and unemployment

For most adults having a job is essential to maintain a decent standard of living. Unemployment almost always means a reduction in income. Until recently unemployment was higher in Scotland, Northern England, Wales and Northern Ireland than in South East England. High unemployment is linked to areas which relied on traditional industries such as coal and shipbuilding. There is also high unemployment in remoter country areas especially the West Highlands and Islands of Scotland due to a lack of industry, because fewer workers are now needed on farms and because tourism is only seasonal. Within Scotland some cities are better off than others. Edinburgh has many white collar jobs in the civil service, insurance and banks whereas Glasgow was more reliant on heavy industry. Aberdeen has low unemployment due to

North Sea oil. Scotland is on the edge of Europe which means we are further away from markets and suppliers and therefore things cost more, are harder to sell and businesses are less keen to set up here.

More recently, unemployment affected southern England as foreign competition and automation led to job losses in engineering and manufacturing such as the car industry in the English Midlands. South East England has had low unemployment due to being near Europe, having many service jobs in civil service, media, communications, many firms head offices and sales etc.

Government policies have also affected the numbers out of work. In the 1980s, the Conservative Government were more concerned to reduce inflation than unemployment which rose to over 3 million. It dropped later in the 1980s for several reasons. The world economy was doing better, the government had set-up various training schemes including youth training and many people who wanted work were no longer included in the official figures (which only show those who are claiming Unemployment Benefit/Jobseekers' Allowance). Also, there were fewer school leavers looking for jobs.

The new century so far has continued the trend started in the 1990s. UK unemployment has fallen and is now lower than in many other European countries. In October 2006, 1.7 million people were unemployed in the UK according to official figures. This equates to about 5.5% of the potential UK workforce. This level is approaching a return to the very low levels between 1945 and the end of the 1970s.

The ways in which the UK Government figures are calculated have been changed many times since 1979. The government said it was necessary so that only those people who were really trying to find work were included in the figures. However, critics of the government claimed it was to reduce the figures to make them look better. There is no doubt that some people who would like permanent jobs are not included in the official figures. For example, a woman who has stopped work for several years to start a family or someone on a training scheme would not be included as they would not be able to claim Jobseekers' Allowance.

Differences among the employed

Income and other benefits derived from work vary greatly. Recent years have seen increasing differences between the incomes of British citizens even among those who have jobs. Recent governments have encouraged the belief that it is good for the country if people have financial incentives to work hard. This meant that many managers receive large pay raises and bonuses. At the same time many low paid workers do not. The government reduced Income

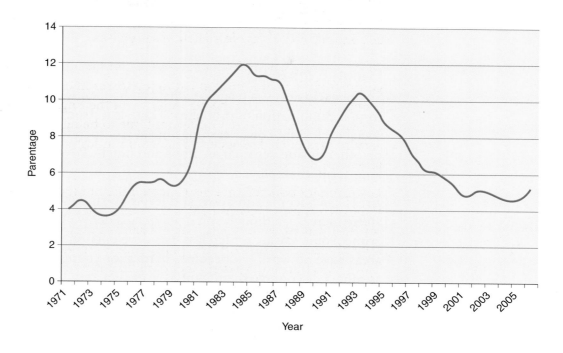

Figure 1.13 UK unemployment rate 1971–2006 →

Source:http://www.esrcsocietytoday.ac.uk/ESRCInfoCentre/facts/index36.aspx?ComponentId=7109&SourcePageId=6971

1   Why is having a job so important?

2   What parts of the UK have traditionally suffered from large levels of unemployment?

3   For what reasons do some areas have higher unemployment than others?

4   Describe differences in unemployment within Scotland.

5   Why has unemployment affected Southern England recently?

6   What has happened to unemployment in the UK in the 1990s?

7   Why has the ways in which the government calculated the unemployment figures been changed? What do critics of the government say about this?

8   Do you think the label 'North–South Divide' is a realistic way to describe unemployment in the UK today?

Tax particularly for the better off. The top rate of Income Tax was reduced from over 80 pence per pound to 40 pence per pound. The fear of unemployment has led many workers to accept low paid work. There has been an increase in part-time working especially by women. There has also been an increase in the number of workers who say they suffer from stress at work often due to the fear of unemployment.

> 1 What has been happening to the differences between the earnings of highly paid and low paid workers? Give reasons for these differences.

Social Exclusion

Social exclusion is a term for what can happen when people or areas suffer from a combination of problems. There is a strong link between poverty and social exclusion. Lower earnings mean less spending and a 'knock-on effect' on other businesses such as shops and hotels. Poverty particularly affects the long-term unemployed.

Areas can become run down and levels of vandalism, crime, drug and alcohol abuse increase, although some politicians deny a link between poverty and crime. Some say an 'underclass' has developed in society when many people in areas have no work – it becomes harder for young people to do well at school as others discourage them. Stress, poor diet and damp housing can cause health problems and family break downs. Houses may be repossessed by building societies if mortgage payments fall behind. New businesses may be reluctant to set up in areas that have acquired a bad reputation.

> 1 What effects can unemployment have on people?
> 2 What effects can unemployment have on communities?

Responses

The Central (UK) Government provides a range of benefits through the DWP. It also provides a range of services designed to move as many people as possible from Welfare into Work.

Figure 1.14 →

What is done to help the unemployed?

If the government spends public money it can create jobs, for example building new roads, schools and hospitals, providing new equipment for the armed forces or cleaning up the environment. The problem with this is that tax would have to be raised to pay for the schemes. The government has a number of schemes to try to find jobs for unemployed people. These include:

- **Jobcentre plus** – part of the DWP. They help people into paid work, give people the help and support they are entitled to if they cannot work and need financial help. They provide information and advice about learning and training opportunities that are offered to help increase someone's chances of finding a job. Jobcentres are located all around the country in most towns and cities and are easily accessible to all.

Figure 1.15 →

- **Training schemes and Apprenticeships** – aimed at young people (16+) who are school leavers who want to combine earning a salary while learning new skills and gaining qualifications. Many employers from a range of industries are helping people to develop in this way.
- **Training for Work** – is a scheme run by Scottish Enterprise to help people find and keep jobs. It provides training support for people who are unemployed (6 months+ and over 25 years old) and actively looking for work. Trainees go on company placements and receive formal training. In many cases, the trainees move into a full-time job.
- **Programme centres** – offer free help with job applications as well as practical advice on looking for jobs, removing barriers to getting and keeping a job, and also for those returning back into the workforce after an illness or raising children. Programme centres provide stamps, stationery, newspapers and access to the internet. Many offer courses to improve interview skills and phone techniques.
- **Flexible working** – Employees who have worked for at least 26 weeks have a statutory right to ask to make an application. Flexible working includes: part-time, flexi-time (choosing when to work around a specific hours you have to work), compressed hours: working agreed hours over fewer days, staggered hours: different starting, breaks and finishing times for employees in the same workplace, job sharing: sharing a job designed for one person with someone else, home working: working from home.
- **Economic development** – Business Link, Business Gateway and Scottish Enterprise offer support by providing advice and information for existing businesses and for people interested in going into business for themselves. Help includes Government grants available, regulations, health and safety information etc.

1   Which UK Government Department is responsible for benefits?

2   Explain what is meant by the phrase from Welfare into Work.

3   Use the headings on page 25 to summarise what each scheme is designed to do and what group it is targeted at.

4   Which benefit do you think is most beneficial? Give a reason to support your answer.

Social Security (DWP) Benefits

The government also provides a number of benefits to help unemployed people. The Labour Government describes its policies for the unemployed as a New Deal. These policies aim to encourage unemployed people to come off welfare and find jobs. There are now New Deals for younger workers, lone parents and others.

Benefits can be universal or selective.

- **Universal** – everyone gets the benefit. The most important universal benefit is Child Benefit. Everyone qualifies for Child Benefit up to the school leaving age of 16; young people who stay on at school continue to receive Child Benefit. The cost of Child Benefit is a concern for the government. The cost could be reduced by making Child Benefit means tested. However, this change would make the government unpopular with parents.
- Selective – these are either:

1   **Contributory** – these benefits are earned by workers paying contributions to the National Insurance scheme. Retirement pension is one of the most important contributory benefits. Unemployment Benefit was another example but this has been replaced by Jobseekers' Allowance which is more complicated. You are entitled to Jobseekers' Allowance for 6 months if you have paid National Insurance. After that it is means tested. Sickness Benefit has been made the responsibility of employer.

2   **Non-Contributory** – these benefits are paid to people who prove they need financial help through some sort of means test. This means you have to prove to the DWP that you need financial help. The most important is Income Support. Other means tested benefits include Tax Credit and Housing Benefit. Most benefits are paid through the DWP. However, Housing Benefit and free school meals are administered by local councils although the money to pay for these comes from the government. Discretionary benefits are paid when an official decides someone needs some form of help. Examples are disability benefits which are based on an assessment of the person's condition.

The advantage of a selective benefit is that it can be targeted at those who need help most. The problem with this is that some people are either too proud to go through a means test or have problems answering questions and filling in forms. This is particularly true of old people. Some old people put their lives at risk especially in the winter as they cannot afford heating but do not want to claim benefits. However, there is also a problem over people who cheat the system and claim benefits they are not entitled to. This can include claiming benefit when you have some sort of job or claiming for dependents such as children you do not have.

Of the £130 billion UK benefit expenditure in 2005/06, nearly £116 billion was managed by the DWP in Great Britain, 65% of which was directed at people of state pension age and over (age 60 for women and 65 for men), 31% was directed at people of working age and 4% at children. However, most of the benefits for working age adults went to families with children.

Source: *Social Trends – 37*

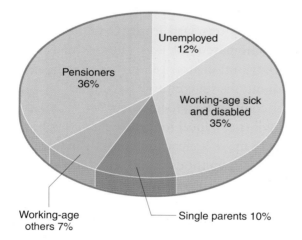

Figure 1.16 Percentage of UK state benefit recipients by reason (2007) →

Source: http://www.poverty.org.uk/06/index.shtml?

1 Summarise the main types of benefits.

2 Give examples of universal and selective benefits.

3 Name two benefits given by Local Councils.

4 Why do some people not claim benefits they are entitled to?

5 Describe the advantages and disadvantages of making benefits selective.

6 Why do some people argue that universal benefits are a waste of money?

7 Use the pie chart shown on page 27 to write a paragraph discussing who is most and least likely to receive state benefits. Can you think of reasons why this is the case?

Universal/non-means tested Welfare Benefit Description

Child Benefit
For up-to-date information and amounts visit:
http://www.hmrc.gov.uk/childbenefit/cb-key.htm

Paid to **all** people who are raising children. It is paid weekly for each child up to the age of 16 years, and continues up to age 18 if the child remains in full-time education. The family's financial situation is not taken into account.

Selective/Means Tested Welfare Benefits Brief Description

Jobseekers Allowance (JSA)	Paid to unemployed people between 18–65 years who are able to work and are seeking work. There are two types of JSA: <ul><li>Contribution-based JSA – for those who have paid sufficient NI contributions, lasts for up to 6 months.</li><li>Income-based JSA – for those who do not qualify for Contribution-based JSA, paid as long as needed as long as the conditions set continue to be met.</li></ul> After completing a form, there is a New Jobseeker Interview with an adviser at a local Jobcentre Plus. A Jobseeker's Agreement is made to make it clear the hours available to work, the kind of work wanted and methods of job searching as well as any training needs or other support required.
Income Support	Available to those who are not available for full-time work and do not have enough money to live on. People eligible for this include single parents, the disabled and carers. If entitled to Income Support the person automatically receives certain other benefits (Housing Benefit, Council Tax Benefit, free dental care, free prescriptions and free school meals).
Housing Benefit	Paid to people on a low income who live in rented accommodation. If a council tenant the Housing Benefit covers this or the benefit can be paid to a private landlord. This benefit is administered by local councils.
Council Tax Benefit	Designed to help people on low incomes pay their Council Tax bill. It is possible to not have to pay any of the bill if on a very low income.
Attendance Allowance	Benefit for people aged 65 years and over who need help with personal care because they are physically or mentally disabled. It is

not affected by the amount of income or savings the person has. The amount is dependent on how much the disability affects the person's life (e.g. requiring help day and night is the higher amount, while just day or night would be the lower). Those under age 65 years may be able to receive Disability Living Allowance.

Bereavement Allowance	After a person becomes a widow/widower they may be entitled to this benefit every week for up to 1 year. If the surviving partner is over age 45 years, not raising any children and under the State Pension age and their late husband/wife paid National Insurance. The older a person is the more they will receive.
Carer's Allowance	A non-contributory benefit paid to men and women who look after a severely disabled person for at least 35 hours a week and so cannot have another job or be in full-time education.
Cold Weather Payment	Paid for each week of very cold weather in a person's area if they already get Pension Credit or other benefits, e.g. Income Support.
Winter Fuel Payment	Paid to those eligible over 60 years to help towards their winter heating costs.
Social Fund	It provides lump sum payments, grants and loans. The amount awarded depends on the individual case – there is no standard amount. Grants are available to cover important costs that are hard to pay for out of your regular income, e.g. a new cooker or washing machine.
Child Tax Credit/ Working tax credit – introduced in 2003 Previously known as Family Credit	Tax credits are payments designed to help with everyday living costs and are based on household circumstances (income, number and age of children, any disabilities). Those who have a child living with them receive Child Tax Credit (CTC) and for those on a low income Working Tax Credit (WTC). The CTC provides support to families for the children and is paid in addition to Child Benefit. The Working Tax Credit allows claimants to 'top up' their earnings. It includes a childcare element to help families who are working and spending money on childcare.
Pension Credit – introduced in 2003	Designed for people aged 60+ years. Pension Credit is extra money given each week to 'top up' pensions
Retirement Pension	A contributory benefit. The amount of basic State Pension received depends on the amount of National Insurance contributions. The State Pension is payable from State Pension age – 65 for men, 60 for women. This will increase to 65 years for women between 2010 and 2020. Individuals may also choose to supplement their state pensions by taking out a company (from where they worked) or a personal pension (available from banks, building societies).

Employment and Support Allowance (ESA)	Employment and Support Allowance will replace Incapacity Benefit and Income Support for new claimants. The new system will consider what an individual is capable of, and what help they need to manage their condition and return to work. Individuals with health conditions will be given support and employment advice to enable them to return to work where possible. ESA will reduce the numbers on benefit but give more money to the genuinely disabled. The capability assessment will also be included.

1 Give examples of contributory and non contributory benefits with a brief summary of each one.

Welfare Reform and Recent Government Initiatives

The cost of the Welfare State has proved much higher than expected and the DWP spends more than any other government department. The National Insurance Scheme has not been sufficient to pay for the cost of social security benefits as well as healthcare. High unemployment has increased the amount paid out in benefits. The largest cost of all has been the increased numbers of elderly people who need pensions and other benefits as well as being the largest single cost for the NHS.

Labour was traditionally seen as more sympathetic to the poor. However, the New Labour Government with Tony Blair as its leader won the 1997 General Election determined not to repeat 1992 when the Tories were able to exploit voters' fears of tax rises to pay for better social security. Blair promised no increase in Income Tax for most people. Labour say they can make Britain a fairer society based on what they call Social Justice through Welfare to Work. New Labour's approach has been to try to move as many claimants as possible into employment.

The government has introduced programmes such as the New Deal, and is now helping people on incapacity benefits through Pathways to Work. It has improved incentives to work by providing greater support through the tax credit system and the introduction of the minimum wage.

The government claim these reforms have led to a significant improvement in the performance of the UK labour market with more people in work than ever before.

This should reduce spending on social security, allow more spending on education and health through increased numbers paying tax and National Insurance.

The New Deal was introduced in 1998. It is divided into a series of programmes for young people, adults, single parents and the disabled. Under the New Deal claimants are encouraged to find jobs or take up training places. They have to be interviewed by advisors to help with this. In addition, there is more help with child care and training and learning opportunities, e.g. for those adults who were not successful at school.

1 What is meant by the term reform?

2 What did the government underestimate when the Welfare State was originally set up?

3 What was the name of new Labour's approach to Welfare reform in 1997?

4 Explain Labour's New Deal programme.

The government aims to have 80% of the adult population in work, to halve child poverty by 2010 and to abolish child poverty entirely by 2020.

Under the new tax credit system, the government pays some benefits through the Inland Revenue into the pay packets of those on low income. There are tax credits for adults in work, for parents and for pensioners. One aim is to create incentives for those on low wages to work rather than live on benefits.

The tax credit system has had problems. Many claimants were over paid and then forced to pay back the money causing more hardship. Other claimants have found delays in receiving their benefit. However, there is evidence that the numbers of people, especially children, living in poverty have been reduced. Around a million children are no longer classed as poor and the government hopes to halve child poverty by 2010.

1 Discuss the advantages and disadvantages of the tax credit system.

The National Minimum Wage (NMW) was resisted by previous Conservative Governments who claimed it would damage British industry. However, most other European countries and even the United States already had minimum wages. It was introduced in the UK for all workers over 18 years of age in 1999. There are now three different minimum wages for those aged 16 to 17 years 18 to 21 years and 22 years and over. The rate was set at a relatively low level as employers claimed they would otherwise make staff redundant. The NMW rates from 1st October 2007 are summarised in Table 2 below.

These rates are reviewed every year and any increase takes place in October of that year. To check the most up to date figures for the NMW visit www.direct.gov.uk.

The NMW has risen by more than the rate of inflation. However, some workers especially women in part-time work still do not receive their appropriate minimum wage. Some are frightened to report it in case they lose their jobs. Underpayment is a particular problem with workers who have recently come into Britain and are unaware of their rights. Other complaints are that the rate is too low especially for young workers. The Low Pay Commission has said that the minimum wage has not led to job losses.

Table 2

16–17 Young People Rate	£3.40
18–21 Development Rate	£4.60
22+ Adult/ Full Rate	£5.52

1   Why was the NMW introduced in 1999?
2   Examine the advantages and disadvantages of the NMW.

The Child Support Agency (CSA) was set up to make parents – usually absent fathers – pay proper maintenance. In practice it was used to try to save the government money and has been discredited. This is to be replaced by Child Maintenance and Enforcement Commission (C-Mec).

Sure Start is a government programme to support families with very young children. It brings together early education, childcare, health and family support.

The aim is to support more deprived communities and vulnerable families. Helping families with very young children means children can fulfil their potential and be in a position to get the most from later opportunities including pre-school education. In Scotland, Sure Start funding of £60 million has been allocated to all 32 local authorities. This recognises the need across Scotland. Visit: www.surestart.gov.uk for more information.

To encourage teenagers to stay in education the Education Maintenance Allowance (EMA) was introduced in 2004. It pays up to £30 per week if young people continue learning/with their studies after age 16 years. The idea is that pupils do not have to worry about money issues and they can concentrate on their studies. EMA claimants can receive £10, £20 or £30 per week depending on household income. Students can also work part-time and the benefits received by parents are not affected. If you have a perfect attendance record, do well and meet your targets then you may receive an extra cash bonus of up to £500.

1   Explain what has happened to the CSA?
2   What groups are Sure Start and EMA targeted at? Why are these groups being targeted by the government?
3   What is your opinion on the EMA?
4   What does the government hope to achieve with Sure Start and the EMA?

Concern over the cost of benefits has lead to changes in pensions. The numbers of years you need to work to qualify for a state pension is being reduced to 30 years for both men and women. This should help women who have had career breaks to start families. However, the pension age will be gradually raised to 68 years by 2046.

Currently, the State Pension age is 65 for men born before 6 April 1959. For women born on or before 5 April 1950, State Pension age is 60. The State Pension age for women born on or after 6 April 1950 will increase gradually to 65 between 2010 and 2020. From April 2020 the State Pension age will be 65 for both men and women.

From 2008, the government wants to make it more difficult for people to be able to claim incapacity benefits by bringing in a tougher test. The new tests will focus on what tasks people can do, such as use a mouse and keyboard, instead of what they cannot do, like lifting something or how far they can walk. It is hoped to cut the number of recipients by up to half. The DWP estimates that about 2.5 million Britons currently claim incapacity benefits. The majority of those currently claiming these benefits suffer from obesity or mental illnesses including stress-related illness. The test is known as the 'new work capability assessment' and will come into effect along with the Employment Support Allowance (ESA). Critics claim this will increase pressure on vulnerable people.

1   Why does the government want people to retire later in life?
2   Explain the changes to incapacity benefit.
3   Why is the government particularly keen on reducing the number of incapacity benefit claimants?

Are responses to poverty working?

In 1999, Tony Blair pledged to eliminate child poverty in the UK 'within a generation'. Ending child poverty can only be achieved by breaking the cycle of deprivation in which people whose childhood was ruined by poverty do less well in school, earn little and, in turn, their children have limited life chances. The first target was to halve child poverty by 2010.

Children's charities calculate that the government is likely to fail in that aim by 900,000 children. The DWP states that 600,000 children have been taken out of poverty since 1997. However, the Institute for Fiscal Studies (IFS) has calculated that it will take a further £3.5–£4 billion in tax credits by the autumn of 2009 to meet the 2010 target. The reduction so far has been achieved by a combination of support for working parents through the tax credit system and schemes to encourage single parents into employment. However, many find the cost of childcare makes it not worth their while to work more than part-time. The system of tax credits for families on lower incomes has proved to be one of those policies which was simple in theory but almost unworkable in practice, largely because the incomes of the poorest are not always predictable; they are often made up of part-time or seasonal work and punctuated by time off to look after children during school holidays. Also there is a low take-up. The charity Barnardo's estimates that one in five families in Scotland are missing out on benefits to which they are entitled. It also requires access to good quality childcare in school holidays and further effort to provide better school meals.

The new Child Poverty Unit works across different government departments, including the Treasury and the DWP plus local councils. In Scotland, there are still 250,000 children (one in four) living in poverty, with high concentrations in some areas, especially in Glasgow and Dundee. Despite the measures already taken, including nursery provision and family centres for pre-school children, many are struggling.

Source: http://www.theherald.co.uk/search/display.var.1794811.0.tackling_child_poverty.php

1 Why do you think Tony Blair chose ending child poverty as one of Labour's main goals?

2 Use the internet to conduct some research to find out if Labour is going to reach this goal?

3 Explain why affordable child care is at the root of the problem.

4 Why has the Child Poverty Unit been set up?

Solutions to inequality

According to the Child Poverty Action Group, a registered charity which works to end child and family poverty in the UK, there are several ways to tackle child poverty. In its 2007 updated publication '*Poverty: the Facts*' several solutions were suggested.

- Provide most for those children at greatest risk of poverty.
- Work towards better jobs, not just more jobs.
- Ensure the safety net protects families against poverty.
- Introduce free at the point of delivery, good-quality childcare.
- Make the reduction of child poverty at the centre of any new child support policies.
- Provide benefit entitlement to all UK residents equally, irrespective of immigration status.
- Reduce the disproportionate burden of taxation on poorer families.
- Improve the quality of delivery and gear it to the needs of the poorest families.

1 Examine recent responses to inequalities.

2 To what extent have government policies reduced inequalities in the UK?

Social Class

Note that in the exam class is seen as background information. You will not be asked detailed questions on how class is defined. You do need to know about the link between social class and inequalities.

Social class is less important now than in the past. Some politicians say that the UK is now a classless society. However, foreign visitors to Britain often comment on the degree to which class still matters in our society. The UK is now much more socially mobile. It is no longer unusual for a person from a working class background to marry someone from the upper classes. Evidence that class is still important comes from the presence of the Royal Family and aristocracy (House of Lords) and the fact that the word is still used so often, although often loosely. Class differences are not just to do with money although that is part of it. If you have enough money you can dress, shop and eat well, send your children to private schools and afford private health care which poorer people cannot. These factors allow you to talk and behave differently. Advertisers, the media and the government themselves all use the concept of class in doing surveys into income and spending patterns. There is a link between class and voting, although this is now weaker. The Conservatives under Mrs Thatcher successfully appealed to voters with working class backgrounds in South East England with policies such as low Income Tax and the right to buy your council house. Labour under Tony Blair distanced itself from Trade Unions and class-based politics as Labour knew it had to win middle class votes in England to win General Elections. More people are now middle class due to the changing job situation. There are more 'white collar' jobs in offices, and far fewer jobs in mines and factories.

1   What do you think social class means? Try to give some examples.

2   Make a list of features of: a) upper class life and b) working class life.

3   What does 'socially mobile' mean?

4   In what ways do people from different social classes behave differently?

5   Who made use of the concept of class? Can you think of a reason for doing this?

6   What is the link between class and voting?

7   Why is the connection between class and voting now less strong?

Definitions of class

Attempts to define class are usually based on occupation.

A distinction is often made between **manual** and **non-manual work**. Manual work is based on physical effort such as labouring or building and is usually seen as working class. Non-manual work does not involve much physical effort and is usually seen as middle class. The terms **blue collar** and **white collar** are sometimes used. They date from traditional work clothing: blue overalls for manual workers and white shirts for non-manual workers in offices and the professions.

The Registrar General's Classification is the official government definition of class.

- Middle Class
  I: Professions and managerial, e.g. architects, doctors, solicitors
  II: Intermediate, e.g. teachers, nurses, farmers
  III: (non-manual): Skilled non-manual, e.g. clerical workers, secretaries, shop assistants.

- Working Class
  III (manual): Skilled manual, e.g. bus drivers, electricians, cooks
  IV: Semi-skilled, e.g. postal workers
  V: Unskilled, e.g. labourers, refuse collectors.

Gender + Race.

[Copy]

work on Monday

UK Parx 50 Over action
on gender inequalities p 50 - 51

what has the gov put
into place and how
effective is it?

There has been some
impact but how much.
could ya up to 55

+ Also use Social Issues in
the gk book

Figure 1.17 →

Another common definition of class is also based on jobs.

The Standard Occupational Classification divides workers into nine groups. Class 1 is managers and administrators in government and large companies. Class 2 covers professionals, e.g. lawyers. Class 5 covers skilled workers. Class 8 is unskilled/semi skilled workers and Class 9 any others not already covered. For a complete list of the classification, visit:

http://www.statistics.gov.uk/methods_quality/soc/structure.asp

Although occupation is the most usual way of measuring social class, it has problems. Very rich people who do not work are not included. Classifications based on occupation ignore the unemployed or housewives. The same job title may mean different things, for example, 'farmer'. A woman's class is that of her husband, although she may be in different class based on her own occupation.

Many say that a woman's class should be based on her own employment not her partner. People could be placed in classes as individuals and not as households. However, in practice family attitudes are likely to be similar.

1 What are definitions of class usually based on?

2 What are the two main types of workers?

3 Describe the government's definition of class?

4 Compare the two classifications of class. Is one better than the other? Give reasons for your answer.

5 What problems arise from using occupation to measure social class?

6 How is a woman's class determined? Why can this be inaccurate?

The growth of the middle class

The middle class is becoming larger. This is linked to changes in the type of work people do. It is also linked to increased living standards.

Traditional working class people are more likely to live in the north of England and Scotland and in council houses, inner city areas or industrial towns. They hold traditional values, for example, in the importance of trade unions and work in declining industries such as shipbuilding and heavy industry, at least when these jobs are still available.

This means that some better off sections of the working class are becoming middle class in values and possession of consumer goods. Other workers, especially in the south of England, are more likely to be homeowners. These workers may be more affluent and more likely to be in jobs in newer industries.

The clear division that used to exist between a working class of manual workers and a middle class of white-collar workers and professionals is no longer appropriate in the UK.

1   Why is the middle class getting larger?

2   Why is there a decline in the number of people who can be described as traditional working class?

Is social class still important?

Some people say Britain is a 'classless' society. However, others argue that class is still important. Evidence that class still matters include:

- **Income differences** – professionals have higher incomes especially in later years as well as better work-related benefits such as pensions, help with housing costs etc.
- **Health** – professionals live longer than unskilled workers. Professional people and their children are less likely to suffer accidental death than those from unskilled manual backgrounds. Manual workers are less likely to have job security and more likely to have earnings linked to hours worked and workplace targets.
- **Education** – the higher a child's social class background, the more chance he or she has of high educational qualifications. Most university students still come from middle class backgrounds.
- **Housing** – nearly all professionals are homeowners compared with under 50% of unskilled manual workers.

1   What evidence can you give to show that social class still matters?

The idea of an underclass

This is a term that has been used to describe a group whose access to life chances is worse than the rest of society. Members of the underclass can include: the long-term unemployed; single parents; the homeless; disadvantaged members of ethnic minority groups; and elderly people living in poverty. The underclass has been blamed for a rise in crime and increases in the number of births outside marriage.

There is concern over the idea of an underclass especially in some deprived housing estates and inner cities where a high proportion of the adults are long-term unemployed. These areas are more likely to offer young people negative values and role models. Children grow up not expecting to work, do badly at school and are likely to drift into crime and drug/alcohol abuse. Local crime rates are high and health below average due to lifestyles and poverty.

1 What is the 'underclass'?

2 Why is there concern with regard to the underclass?

Gender Inequality

Background

Fewer people live in the traditional family of a married couple with dependent children. Many more people are living on their own: around one in ten adults and around 30% of households are made up of one person.

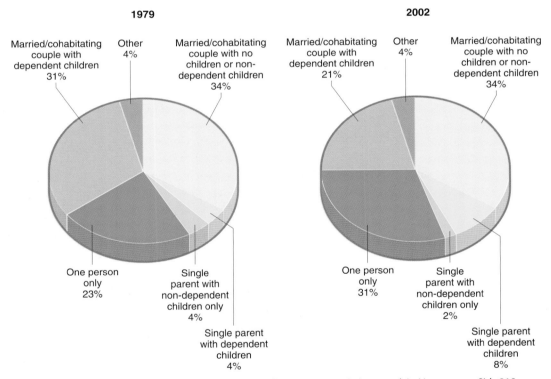

1979

Married/cohabiting couple with dependent children
31%

Other 4%

Married/cohabiting couple with no children or non-dependent children
34%

One person only
23%

Single parent with non-dependent children only
4%

Single parent with dependent children
4%

2002

Married/cohabiting couple with dependent children
21%

Other 4%

Married/cohabiting couple with no children or non-dependent children
34%

One person only
31%

Single parent with non-dependent children only
2%

Single parent with dependent children
8%

Figure 2.1 Types of households in the UK (1979 and 2002) →

Source: http://www.statistics.gov.uk/cci/nugget.asp?id=818

Some women do not have children either by choice or because they are not able to have children. Although the proportion of women who do not have children has increased to 25%, the majority of women still see having at least one child as an important part of their lives. Women who do become mothers are now older when they give birth and are also opting for smaller families. In recent years, it has become more socially acceptable for women not to have children. This may be due to the fact that it is more common to remain childless and perhaps focus on a career instead.

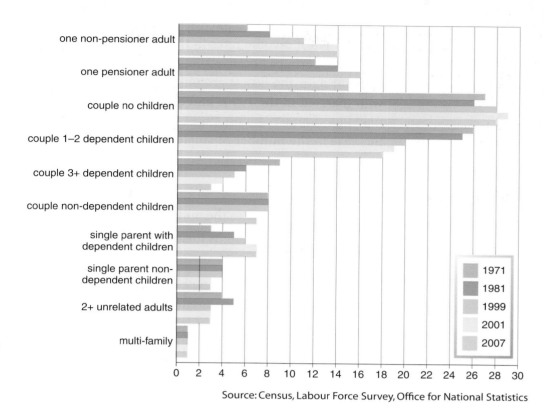

Figure 2.2 UK households by type of family (1971–2007) →

one non-pensioner adult
one pensioner adult
couple no children
couple 1–2 dependent children
couple 3+ dependent children
couple non-dependent children
single parent with dependent children
single parent non-dependent children
2+ unrelated adults
multi-family

1971
1981
1999
2001
2007

0 2 4 6 8 10 12 14 16 18 20 22 24 26 28 30

Source: Census, Labour Force Survey, Office for National Statistics

Most people prefer to have smaller families than in the past; few families now have four or more children. The birth rate now averages less than two children per mother. People are getting married at older ages as women postpone having children. The average age for having a baby is now 28. There are about 3% more male than female births every year. However, because of the higher mortality of men at all ages, there is a turning point at about 50 years of age. After this age the number of women is higher than the number of men.

1 What has happened to the size of families?
2 Why are there fewer traditional families than there used to be?
3 Explain why people now have less children.
4 Why are some women choosing not to have any children?
5 Why are couples getting married later and women choosing to delay motherhood?

The number of marriages has fallen in recent years. In 2005, there was a 10% fall in the number of marriages across the UK since 2004. First marriages have declined by nearly a half compared with 1970. Over a third of marriages are remarriages of one or both partners. Men are more likely than women to remarry after separation. 74% of households with dependent children are headed by a married/cohabiting couple compared with 92% in 1971. 24% of families are headed by single mothers.

Separation and divorce have become much more common and Britain has one of the highest divorce rates in the European Union. Divorce rates for Scotland are lower perhaps because a higher proportion of Scots attend church. Cohabiting is the fastest growing family type. Around two-thirds of women who married in the 1990s had cohabited with their future husband before marriage compared with 4% of those married in 1966. There has been an increase in the number of single parents. The tendency of children to stay with their mothers on separation means that at least nine in ten single parents are women.

> 1   Describe changes in the number and types of marriages.
>
> 2   Are most single parents men or women? Can you explain this?

The role of women has been changing. The traditional distinction between the woman's role of homemaker and the man's role of breadwinner has been eroded. Modern family planning methods have made it far easier for women to choose the timing and spacing of their children and limit the number of children that they have. Women have been postponing child bearing. In 1992, for the first time, women in their early thirties were more likely to give birth than women in their early twenties.

> 1   In what ways have women's roles changed?

Evidence

Note that evidence and reasons overlap.

Evidence for continued gender inequalities comes from a number of studies and surveys. Recently, the Women and Work Commission reported that the median gender pay gap still exists although it has reduced from 17.4% in 1997 to 12.6% in 2007. The mean figure has fallen from 20.7% to 17.2% in the same period. The median part-time gender pay gap has remained fairly static and has reduced from 43.5% in 1997 to 39.1% in 2007. The mean figure for 2007 is 35.6%, compared with 41.9% in 1997.

The gender pay gap means that women's abilities and skills are not being fully utilised in businesses and the economy. In spite of the increasing participation of women in the labour market, marked differences still exist compared with men. Women tend to work in clerical and secretarial occupations, personal service and sales, as well as outnumbering men in health and education. Even within those industries in which women predominate they tend to have the less prestigious jobs. For example, only three in ten secondary school head teachers are women although almost half of secondary school teachers are women. However, women are making inroads into some traditionally male professions – there are now more women than men solicitors aged 30 years or under.

The tendency for women to work in low status, low paid jobs is reflected in their earnings. At all ages women earn less, on average, than men. The peak age for earnings among women full-time employees is earlier than for men; in their early thirties instead of the early forties. This may be a result of women being more likely to take career breaks to have children, which has a bad effect on their careers and causes their earning power to fall, as they tend not to return at the same level of responsibility. In only 13% of couples where both partners are in full-time work do the women earn at least £50 per week more than the man.

Nearly two-thirds of the poorest pensioners are women. 85% of men are entitled a full-state pension compared with 30% of women. This is due to women taking time away from work to raise families.

1 Compare the types of jobs women and men tend to have.

2 Explain why women's unequal participation in the labour force can have a damaging effect on the UK's economy.

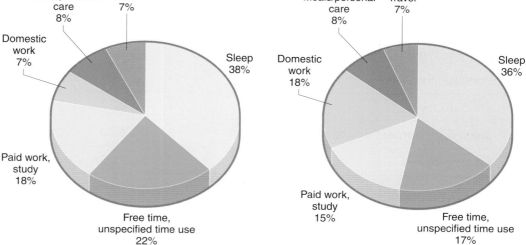

Household without children

Meals/personal care 8%
Travel 7%
Domestic work 7%
Sleep 38%
Paid work, study 18%
Free time, unspecified time use 22%

Household with children

Meals/personal care 8%
Travel 7%
Domestic work 18%
Sleep 36%
Paid work, study 15%
Free time, unspecified time use 17%

Figure 2.3 Average time spent by families with and without children in the UK (2006) →

Source: http://news.bbc.co.uk/1/hi/uk/7071611.stm

Table 3 Weekly median earnings, full-time and part-time employees, 1997 and 2005, (£)

	1997	2005
Weekly pay (£/week)		
All males	328.1	417.6
All females	186.8	268.5
Women's pay as % of men's	56.9	64.3
Full-time males	340.8	447.8
Full-time females	247.0	362.1
Women's pay as % of men's	72.5	80.9
Part-time males	80.0	115.2
Part-time females	94.4	137.4
Women's pay as % of men's	118.0	119.3

Source: Annual Survey of Hours and Earnings, http://www.statistics.gov.uk/ StatBase/Product.asp?vlnk=13101

Table 4 Gross median hourly earnings (£) by occupational group, excl. overtime, in Scotland in 2005

Occupational group	All Employees	Male	Female	Earnings ratio %
Professional	17.14	17.79	16.70	94
Managers & Senior Officials	15.49	16.86	13.45	80
Assoc Professional & Technical	12.54	12.70	12.37	97
Skilled Trades	8.95	9.14	6.03	66
Administrative & Secretarial	8.05	8.67	7.95	92
Process, Plant & Machine Ops.	7.71	8.00	6.23	78
Personal Service	7.12	7.69	7.04	92
Elementary	5.87	6.57	5.50	84
Sales & Customer Service	5.66	6.00	5.57	93
All employees	9.07	10.07	8.26	82

Source: Annual Survey of Hours and Earnings. C. Young (2006) *Low Pay in Scotland*. http://www.slpu.org.uk/

1   Write a paragraph to summarise the evidence found in the statistics shown.

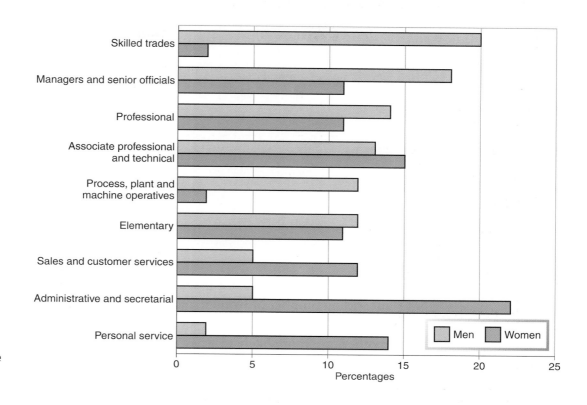

Figure 2.4 The types of jobs done by men and women in the UK (2005) →

Source: http://www.statistics.gov.uk/cci/nugget.asp?id=1654

Reasons

Traditional roles for men and women

During the early part of the twentieth century the roles of husbands and wives within the home were separate and unequal. It was generally thought that married women were expected to take the main responsibility for housework and childcare. Married men were expected to be the main wage earners. Women's roles differed, however, according to social class. In addition to housework and childcare, many working-class women went out to work or took on paid work from home such as doing laundry. Among the middle class, on the other hand, the wife was not expected to undertake paid work. She supervised the work of household employees such as maids and nannies. Families were male dominated and both working- and middle-class husbands were expected to provide for their family. They were also expected to take the important decisions and that their family would respect and obey them. These attitudes have been changing but slowly. Many older people – women as well as men – are still not convinced that women and men should be able to do the same work or that men should help with doing the housework.

Figure 2.5 →

A fundamental change in the United Kingdom workforce has been the increasing number of women, particularly those who work part time. The proportion of mothers who go to work has also increased, although married mothers are more likely to work than single mothers.

Women today are more likely than their mothers to have educational qualifications. The number of women in post-education has increased at a faster rate than that for men, although much of the increase has been in part-time education. Lack of qualifications has an effect on income; the unemployment rate for women with no qualifications is almost four times that for a woman educated above A level/Higher standard. Men with no qualifications have even higher unemployment rates than women.

Although women are still not fully equal with men at work the fact that many women now have jobs, or even careers, has led to a considerable change in women's attitudes. Nowadays most women, especially younger women, reject stereotypes of 'a woman's place'. However, it is also true that many working women still have to do most of the housework.

1 Describe the traditional roles of men and women.
2 What has been happening to the number of women who have jobs?
3 Compare the types of jobs men and women have.
4 Why are there relatively few women in top jobs?
5 What has happened to the number of girls who go on to further education? Why is this important?
6 In what ways can having a job influence a woman's attitudes?
7 Are household duties shared equally by men and women?

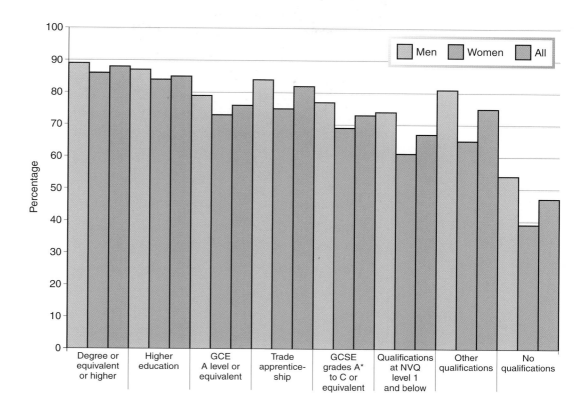

Figure 2.6 UK employment rates by sex and education qualifications (2007) ➡

Source: Labour Force Survey, Office for National Statistics

1 Examine the changing role of women in UK society.

2 Assess the evidence for continued gender inequality in the UK.

Direct and Indirect Discrimination

Most people understand direct discrimination. An example is when an employer avoids employing a woman because they think she will be more likely to take time off work to look after children. Some employers will only employ older women who are unlikely to have children. In some areas of work there is still a prejudice against women. Many men still do not accept women can do physically demanding jobs such as building or work shifts. Sometimes this is put forward as concern for the woman's safety. Despite efforts by senior managers, there is evidence that in the armed forces, police and fire and prison services many men resent women or think that they can only carry out a limited range of tasks. Note that there are a few jobs where it is still legal to specify male or female staff, e.g. children's homes.

Indirect discrimination occurs where certain requirements are imposed by an employer which is unfair on one sex. Indirect discrimination generally occurs when a rule or condition, which is in theory applied to everyone, can be met by a much smaller proportion of people from a particular group. Jobs demanding a certain length of service or experience make it hard for women who have had career breaks to start families. The ability to work full-time or shifts or do extra hours when needed can be difficult for women with small children. Jobs which demand physical requirements, e.g. height, discriminate against women.

1   Give an example of what is meant by direct and indirect discrimination.
2   Apart from children's homes, can you think of any other jobs where it is legal to specify male or female staff.
3   What obstacles do some women have when looking for a job or promotion?

Responses

Laws to create equal opportunities

A number of laws have been passed to try to ensure equal rights. The 1970 Equal Pay Act says all workers should get the same pay for the same work.

The Sex Discrimination Act of 1975 said that employers cannot refuse someone a job, promotion or the chance to get training, buy a house etc. because of their sex (with a few exceptions, e.g. children's homes, armed forces, priesthood).

The Employment Protection Act said that a woman cannot lose her job because she is pregnant and has the right to return to work after the birth.

In 2007, the new Equality and Human Rights Commission (EHRC) combined the work of the Equal Opportunities Commission, the Commission for Racial Equality and the Disability Rights Commission. The remit of the EHRC is to work to eliminate discrimination, reduce inequality and protect human rights ensuring that everyone has a fair chance to participate in society. The new commission also takes on the responsibility for other aspects of equality: age, sexual orientation and religion or belief, as well as human rights. The Equality and Human Rights Commission is a non-departmental public body established under the Equality Act 2006. This means it is accountable for its public funds, but is independent of the government.

The EHRC employs lawyers who are specialists in equality law so the EHRC are able to take legal action on behalf of individuals especially if there are cases that will clarify and improve existing laws. Although they cannot take on every individual case, help is also available to individuals online and through a helpline. The Commission monitors the performance of the government to ensure it is on track to fulfil its commitment to promote a fair and equal society. The Commission liaises with government departments and provides guidance and advice to organisations. It wishes to use the media to highlight issues with the public and to provide education and information to the public. Every 3 years, the Commission will present a 'state of the nation' report to be presented to Parliament.

1   What is the remit of the EHRC?

2   The EHRC is a non-departmental public body, what does this mean?

Task visit: www.equalityhumanrights.com

Other measures to promote gender equality

The Gender Equality Duty (GED) was the biggest change to sex equality legislation in 30 years and is expected to have a major impact on central and local government in Scotland and the rest of the UK. The GED came into force in April 2007. It requires public organisations to promote gender equality and eliminate sex discrimination instead of the old system which relied on complaints from individuals. Public bodies will have to show they are encouraging equality, e.g. by making sure adverts and working practices do not favour one sex. The GED will also apply to companies which supply the public sector.

Within the civil service and many other public services there are now targets for the proportion of women in certain positions. For example, by 2008 30% of top management posts in the civil service should be held by women.

1   Make a summary of the Gender Equality Duty (GED).

Statutory Maternity Pay (SMP) provides mothers with money to allow them to take time off before and after the birth of their baby. Recently, changes to the Work and Families Act mean that SMP is now paid for 39 weeks (previously 26 weeks). However, there are conditions: the woman must have been in employment for at least 26 weeks. SMP pays 90% of earnings.

Additional Paternity Leave and Pay have been introduced to encourage fathers to participate more in looking after their children. From April 2009, fathers will be able to take up to 26 weeks leave with statutory paternity pay if the mother returns to work.

Figure 2.7 →

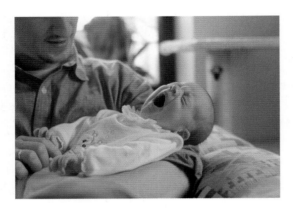

Childcare is crucial to many working families. All 3 and 4 year olds are now entitled to free, part-time government-funded early education for 12.5 hours per week. By 2010, all children between 3 and 14 years old will qualify for year round childcare from 8 a.m. to 6 p.m. every weekday.

Figure 2.8 →

A number of social security benefits help women and families. Lower and even middle income families are helped by Working Tax Credits; all families receive Child Benefit. Pension Credits have helped 2 million pensioners, mostly women. Carer's Credit is particularly helpful to women as most carers are female.

The New Deal for Lone Parents

Single parents can join this scheme if they are bringing up children as a single parent, if their youngest child is under 16 years old and they are not working, or working less than 16 hours per week. It is a voluntary programme designed to support single parents moving into work. A personal advisor will help the single parent to find and apply for jobs, offer practical advice and financial support to help find suitable childcare and training opportunities.

The NMW has benefited more women than men as women are more likely to be in low paid work. Flexible working is now a right where children are disabled or under 6 years of age. Over 5 million UK workers work through some form of flexible working arrangement.

The number of women in UK Parliament is higher than ever but still well under 50%. The law now allows political parties special measures to increase the number of female candidates.

Other laws allow female victims of domestic abuse to keep homes (the man is now evicted) and there is more support for victims of domestic violence. The UK Government has signed the European Convention against Human Trafficking which tries to locate and help women brought into the UK illegally.

1   Make a summary of the laws designed to create equal opportunities for women.
2   Choose one law that you think has the most impact on working women.

Has equality been achieved?

Women are still not fully equal to men despite these laws. Main reasons are:

- Continued direct discrimination by some men.
- The difficulty of proving sex discrimination cases where a woman has to prove it was her gender and no other reason that caused her problem.
- The reluctance of many women to take an employer to an industrial tribunal as they may then look for an excuse to sack her later.
- Many women are reluctant to push themselves forward due to the demands of family life, lack of confidence, the effects of stereotyping at home and in school.

However, this situation is now changing. Girls outperform boys at school and in higher education. Females are now more common as managers and in previously male-dominated jobs, such as engineering, the police and driving. It takes time for women to reach top managerial positions but this is likely to become easier over the next 20 years. Some jobs are still tougher for women to break into than others such as the law, finance and business.

Figure 2.9 →

Child care is still a major factor in whether a woman can continue her career. Often women take jobs to suit families even if this means part-time or less skilled work than when they were single. The UK is only now catching up with the rest of Western Europe in the provision of child care. Government policy is now to provide nursery places for all 3 and 4 year olds. Many women still have to pay for some child care, a particular problem for women on low pay and single parents.

Cracks in the 'glass ceiling'?

- Girls now outperform boys at all stages of education.
- Girls are now entering traditional male jobs, for example, engineering.
- Increased numbers of girls entering all the professions even those traditionally seen as male-dominated jobs, i.e. law, accounting.
- Increasing numbers of female managers who in time will move to senior positions.
- More women elected to the House of Commons and the other parliaments/councils around the UK.
- More effective laws and procedures.

Some politicians and many employers are reluctant to improve women's legal rights at work. They argue that giving women – or other workers – too many rights is bad for the economy. They also argue that target setting means that jobs will no longer go to the best candidate. When the European Union forced Britain to have the same retirement age for men and women, the government raised it to 65 years for all instead of reducing it to 60 years to save money.

When Gordon Brown became British Prime Minister in June 2007 he created a new Government Department and named a Secretary of State for Children, Schools and Families.

Women are still under-represented in the ranks of power, policy and decision making, despite the advances which have been made in recent years. The 1997 General Election was the first ever when over 100 female MPs were elected. At present there are 126 female MPs making up 20% of all MPs. After the 2007 elections to local councils in Scotland, 22% of all local councillors were females. In the Scottish Parliament, females are better represented with 44 females out of the total 129 MSPs (34%); however, it is still well below half.

Figure 2.10 →

Figure 2.11 →

1 What is meant by the term 'glass ceiling'?

2 Why are women still not entirely equal to men?

3 What evidence is there that this is now changing?

4 In what ways can the availability of child care affect a woman's career?

5 Describe women's progress in politics.

1 Examine the success of responses to promote gender equality.

Inequalities and ethnicity

Background

For centuries people from other countries have settled in Britain, either to escape political or religious oppression or in search of better economic opportunities. In the past, most were people from European countries, especially Ireland, leaving their own countries to look for a better life or escape persecution. In the twentieth century people from the Caribbean and Southern Asia entered Britain. In recent years, the number of people coming from Southern Asia has continued but there has been a rise in immigration from some African countries such as Ghana, Nigeria and Somalia. It has been estimated that since 1997, 1.1 million foreign workers have come to the UK. Figures from the Office of National Statistics estimate that around 8% of the UK workforce is foreign. The DWP have reported that just under half of the 1.1 million foreign workers were from the EU, the remainder came from non-EU and Commonwealth countries such as Australia, Canada, New Zealand, South Africa with others from the United States.

The 2001 census reported that that 92% of the population said they belonged to the 'White' group, while only 8% described themselves as belonging to another ethnic group or considered themselves to be 'Mixed' race. The largest group was Indians followed by Pakistanis, mixed ethnicity, Black Caribbeans, Black Africans and Bangladeshis. The remaining ethnic groups made up the remaining 0.5% of the population.

Today's United Kingdom has never been as culturally diverse as it is at present. In 2001, 8.3% of the population were overseas. Table 5 on page 56 shows the number of ethnic minority groups in the UK according to the 2001 Census data (Office of National Statistics), which is becoming increasingly out of date. The next census is due to be carried out in 2011.

1 Give examples of some of the countries that foreign workers to UK come from.
2 Why can the UK be described as a culturally diverse society?
3 Summarise the main features of the UK's population in 2001.
4 If you were to update the figures for today what do you think they might look like? Give reasons to back up your points.

Figure 3.1 ➡

Not only is the ethnic minority population small but an increasing proportion (now just below half) was born in Britain. Compared with white people, a higher proportion was under 16 years but a much lower proportion was over pensionable age.

Members of ethnic minority groups are heavily concentrated in industrial and urban areas, and over half live in South East England, especially in London; 60% of Black Britons live in London. Over 10% of the ethnic population lives in the West Midlands while North East England and South West England have the lowest populations with around 2%.

In the 1950s and 1960s staff shortages in public services such as transport and the NHS led to advertising campaigns in parts of the British Commonwealth. Black people from the West Indies came to settle mainly in London and some other English cities. More than half of this group are now born in Britain. However, the group as a whole has not been as upwardly mobile as some others. Movement of Black Africans into the UK has been more recent; mainly since the 1970s. As more recent arrivals, a smaller percentage of Black Africans are British born (about 1 in 3) compared to Black West Indians. Immigrants from Africa come from a variety of countries, many from former British colonies. Some are political refugees, many are students. Skill levels tend to be high, around 1 in 4 are potentially professionals.

The Indian community is the largest non-white minority in the UK; around 1 in 6 of the total minority population. Some of this group came from East Africa and 1 in 3 are in professional jobs.

Table 5 **UK Population by Ethnic Group, April 2001**

Main group	Sub-group	Proportion of the British Population	Ethnic Minority Population
White (includes White Irish and White Other)	White British	92.1%	n/a
All ethnic minorities (see breakdown below)		7.9%	
Asian or Asian British	Indian Pakistani Bangladeshi Other Asian	1.8% 1.3% 0.5% 0.4%	22.7% 16.1% 6.1% 5.3%
Black or Black British	Black Caribbean Black African Black Other	1.0% 0.8% 0.2%	12.2% 10.5% 2.1%
Chinese	Chinese	0.4%	5.3%
Other		0.4%	5.0%
Mixed Race			
White & Black Caribbean		all groups together 1.2%	
White & Black African			
White & Asian			
Another mixed background			

Source: UK Census 2001

Bangladeshis have been less successful economically. Many work in catering: 'Indian' restaurants are often run by Bangladeshis. The Pakistani community have also been less economically successful than Indians. However, this varies between regions. In Scotland, a higher proportion of Pakistanis are self-employed than in the North of England. Around half of Asians living in Britain were born in this country. Cultural differences in dress and religion have lead to tensions although more so in several English cities than in Scotland.

A relatively small Chinese community has lived in the UK for many years. Numbers have increased recently; some coming from Hong Kong when it was handed back to communist China. A high portion of this community are professional and self-employed.

Figure 3.2 An article encouraging Barbadians to work in the London transport network was printed in the *Barbados Advocate* in June 1962 →

1 In which regions of the UK do ethnic minority groups tend to live?

2 Rank the Asian communities in terms of their economic success.

3 Suggest reasons why some ethnic minorities have found it difficult to integrate into UK society.

Immigration

It is wrong to think that anyone can come to Britain to stay. The immigration rules are strict. Until recently only UK citizens had the automatic right to come into the country. As we are now in the European Union, EU citizens can come to Britain and British people can go to any of the other 27 EU countries.

Most immigrants to the UK are white. Until recently most came from Commonwealth countries, such as Australia, New Zealand, Canada, or the USA. In some cases they were born in the UK and had settled for some time abroad but decided to return.

When the UK joined what is now the European Union in 1973 immigrants from Europe increased. It has increased considerably now that so many East European countries are members. It is one of the principles of the EU that citizens of any country can move to and look for work in any member state. However, there are restrictions on numbers of workers from the most recent members such as Bulgaria and Romania. The level of immigration and its effect on the UK are controversial. There have been problems in estimating how many people have come to the UK recently and how many of them entered illegally. Most economists say that immigrants who are mostly young adults looking for work help the British economy as they take jobs local people do not want. However, they put a strain on public services such as the NHS and housing. The government has revised its figures for the number of foreign nationals working in the UK since 1997 – from 800,000 to 1.1 million. The extra 300,000, found after analysis of the Labour Force Survey, shows 8% of the UK's 29.1 million workforce are foreign. Research by the Home Office reported that after the expansion of the European Union from 2004–2007, 796,000 Eastern Europeans have applied to work in the UK, 766,000 applications were approved.

Figure 3.3 Member countries of the EU (2007) →

1 Create a table stating the good and bad points about immigration to the UK.

2 Where do a large number of immigrants come from? Give reasons to explain your choice.

2008 marked a turning point in how the UK Government determines who from outside the EU can and cannot come to the UK to work and study. The new system is similar to the Australian-style points-based immigration system (PBS). To qualify, applicants must earn a certain number of points in various categories such as education, income, ability to speak English etc. The new regulations mean that only those migrants with the right skills for the British economy needs will be able to come to the UK to work and study. The government recognises that highly skilled migrants are vital to Britain. They tend to be highly educated, do essential jobs and pay tax. The government hopes the new system will simplify the previous system to help the Home Office to control migration, tackle abuse of the immigration laws and identify the most talented applicants. Employers will still act as sponsors as in the old system.

There are five tiers in the UK's new immigration system:

- Tier 1: Highly skilled individuals who will contribute to growth and productivity.
- Tier 2: Skilled workers with a job offer to fill gaps in United Kingdom work force.
- Tier 3: Limited numbers of low skilled workers needed to fill temporary labour shortages.
- Tier 4: Students.
- Tier 5: Youth mobility and temporary workers: people allowed to work in the United Kingdom for a limited period of time to satisfy non-economic objectives (working holidays for students and young people).

Figure 3.4 →

The other main political parties are sceptical of the new plans. The Conservatives feel that there should be an annual limit placed on the number of immigrants allowed into the UK. They feel it would help to lessen the pressure on housing, schools and social services. The Liberal Democrats say the rules could lead to skills shortages. This is because workers with less skills, for example those who work in Chinese or Indian restaurants, would not score enough points to be admitted.

1 What changes were made to the UK's immigration policy in 2008?

2 What does the new policy hope to achieve according to the government?

3 Give a few ideas of the sorts of topics the points-based test might cover.

4 Summarise the five tiers of the new immigration system.

5 Can you think of any jobs where foreign workers are essential?

6 What do the main political parties say about the immigration system?

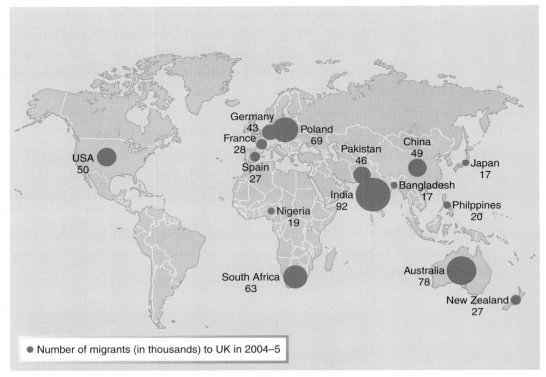

Figure 3.5 Top 15 countries people emigrate to the UK from, in thousands (2004–2005) →

● Number of migrants (in thousands) to UK in 2004–5

Germany 43
Poland 69
France 28
Pakistan 46
China 49
USA 50
Spain 27
Japan 17
Bangladesh 17
India 92
Philppines 20
Nigeria 19
South Africa 63
Australia 78
New Zealand 27

Source: http://news.bbc.co.uk/1/hi/uk_politics/7068291.stm

Who is the typical migrant worker?

(according to Home Office statistics June 2006)

They are one of more than 427,000 who have successfully applied for work in the UK; they are likely to be Polish (62%), aged between 18–34 years (82%) work in a factory (56%) and settle in the East Anglia region of England which has the highest proportion of migrant workers (15%).

Figure 3.6 Migrant workers in Cambridgeshire →

Figure 3.7 Asylum seekers are held at detention centres such as the one in Dungeval →

Asylum Seekers

Asylum means people asking permission to come to a country to escape persecution. All countries, including the UK, have traditionally accepted genuine refugees. Some UK politicians now say that many asylum seekers are now wanting entry to Britain for economic reasons (to improve their living standards) instead of more political factors. The number of applicants seeking asylum saw a huge drop in 1996 with the announcement that asylum seekers would not be eligible to claim social security benefits. In 2006, 23,610 asylum applications were made with an estimated 26% (6225) of these granted. In 2006, the main nationalities applying for asylum were people from Eritrea, Afghanistan, Iran, China and Somalia. In 2007, applications for those seeking asylum to the UK were at their lowest levels in 14 years.

1 What does asylum mean?

2 Why do some UK politicians want to reduce the number of people given asylum in Britain?

3 What happened when social security was withdrawn from asylum seekers?

Who are UK citizens?

British citizenship is given automatically at birth to a child born in Britain if his or her mother or father is a British citizen. A child born abroad to a British citizen is a British citizen. British citizens can leave and enter Britain as they wish.

People from Britain's few remaining colonies and some other people with United Kingdom connections are called British citizens but they do not have the automatic right to come to Britain to stay. They can apply to become full British citizens after 5 years' residence in Britain. However, people from Gibraltar and the Falkland Islands can come to stay in Britain whenever they like. Special arrangements were made to allow a small number of Chinese people from Hong Kong to become British citizens when Hong Kong was given back to China.

All other adults aged 18 years or over have to apply for naturalisation. Naturalisation is at the government's discretion. Someone applying has to live in the UK for 5 years, or 3 years if their husband or wife is British.

Foreigners can visit the UK for holidays and to carry out legitimate business. However, they cannot settle in the UK without permission. Citizens of the European Union, Norway and Iceland have the right to come to Britain to work or study.

Source: http://www.homeoffice.gov.uk/rds/pdfs07/hosb1407.pdf

1 Examine the benefits of immigration to the UK.

Evidence

Note that evidence and reasons overlap.

The poverty rate varies substantially between ethnic groups: Bangladeshis (65%), Pakistanis (55%) and Black Africans (45%) have the highest rates; Black Caribbeans (30%), Indians (25%), White Other (25%) and White British (20%) have the lowest rates. For all ethnic groups, the income poverty rate appears to have fallen over the last decade at a roughly similar rate.

Source: http://www.poverty.org.uk/reports/ethnicity%20findings.pdf

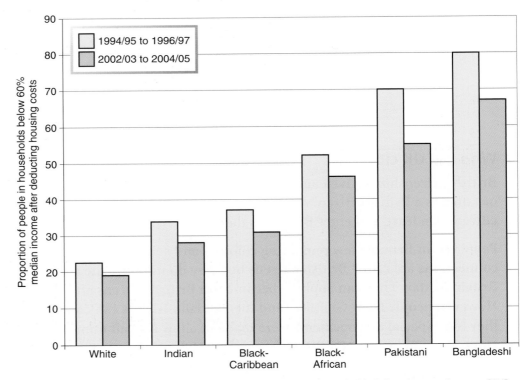

Figure 3.8 Proportion of people from each ethnic group living below median 60% income 1994/95–96/97 and 2002/03–04/05) ➔

Source: Households Below Average Income, DWP

As seen in Figure 3.8 above, unemployment varies significantly between ethnic groups. Black Caribbean males had the highest rates of unemployment in 2004. Pakistani women were by far the group most likely to be unemployed. White British and White Irish had the lowest figures in both male and females categories.

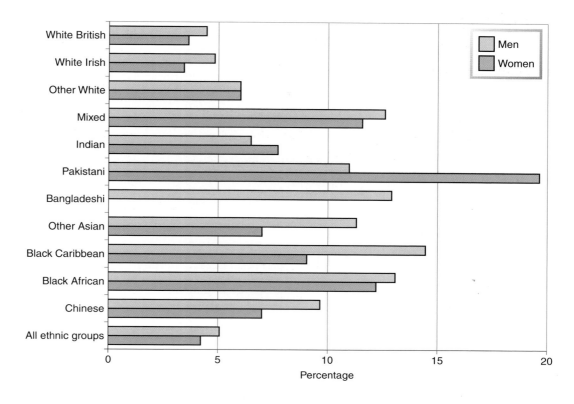

**Figure 3.9
Unemployment in
the UK by ethnic
group and sex
(2004)** →

Source: http://www.statistics.gov.uk/CCI/nugget.asp?ID=462&Pos=6&ColRank=2&Rank=12

Home ownership

The data in Figure 3.10 on page 64 gives figures for 2001. It shows Indians were the most likely of any of the different ethnic groups to own their own homes (76%) in Great Britain. White British (70%) and Pakistani (67%) households were the next most likely to do so. Black African, Other Black and Bangladeshi households were the least likely to own their own homes with only 26% of Black African households doing so.

---

1 What evidence is there to indicate that inequalities exist among ethnic groups in the UK?

---

1 To what extent do ethnic minorities experience disadvantage?

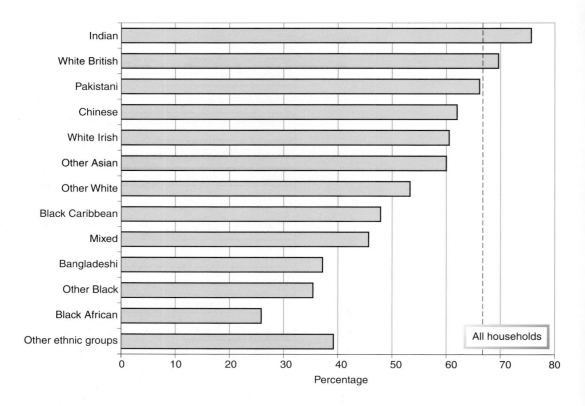

Figure 3.10 Percentage of ethnic groups in the UK who own their own home (2001) →

Source: http://www.statistics.gov.uk/CCI/nugget.asp?ID=1699&Pos=2&ColRank=2&Rank=10002001

Reasons

Evidence that racism is a problem in Britain comes from surveys into the experiences of ethnic minorities. Most report experiencing at least some form of racism, often in the form of name calling or other abuse. Many people have also experienced more serious racism such as threats, actual violence or persecution such as graffiti on the walls of houses, dirt or threatening letters put through doors. Young people may find it more difficult to succeed at school and leave school with fewer qualifications. The fact that ethnic minorities tend to live in poorer parts of inner cities and have below average incomes suggests that they find it harder than white people to get a decent job or achieve promotion. Some people argue that the failure of the government to do more to help ethnic minorities is itself a form of racism as are the immigration laws.

1 What reasons are given to explain why ethnic minorities do less well in society?

Responses

Central government and local authorities have a range of policies in place to try and reduce discrimination. There are various types of grants which are designed to put resources into projects which will benefit ethnic minorities. An example of this is when specialist teachers are employed to help children who do not speak English as their first language.

The police are keen to recruit from ethnic minorities especially in cities where there are ethnic minority communities. However, young people from some ethnic minorities are reluctant to join the police. Despite efforts by senior police officers there is evidence of racism by some police officers in the way they have dealt with Blacks and Asian people.

Figure 3.11 ➡

The government is promoting equal opportunities in the workplace and has introduced training programmes for unemployed people. The greatest demand seems to be for people who need training in English as a second language.

1 What evidence is there of members of ethnic minorities achieving success?
2 What sort of projects can the government and local councils provide to help ethnic minorities?
3 Why are the police keen to recruit from the Black and Asian communities?

Laws and initiatives to improve race relations

The Race Relations Act of 1976 made discrimination unlawful on the grounds of colour, race, nationality or ethnic or national origin when dealing with employment, housing, education and advertising. The act has been updated giving public authorities a statutory duty to promote race equality. The Race Relations (Amendment) Act 2000 included an obligation for public authorities, including the police, to eliminate racial discrimination, ensure equal opportunities and to promote good race relations.

1 What does the Race Relations Act say?

2 Which group was included in the 2000 Amendment Act?

The Commission for Racial Equality (CRE) was established in 1976 but was replaced by the Equality and Human Rights Commission (EHRC) in 2007. It was established under the Equality Act 2006. The EHRC is responsible for enforcing the law, helping to build better relations, lobbying and campaigning in order to achieve a more integrated society, promote and publish best practice to help employees and employers alike. The EHRC is also able to use its enforcement powers, where necessary, to guarantee equality. Visit: www.equalityhumanrights.com to find out more.

1 What has the CRE been replaced by?

2 What are the aims of the EHRC?

The Crime and Disorder Act 1998 allows extra penalties if an offence is racially aggravated, for example when an assault is clearly racial.

A Public Service Agreement means that all government departments have to include racial equality targets as part of their plans. They have to show that they are promoting equality and monitoring it. There are targets in education, health, employment and housing.

The police have a duty to promote diversity and are keen to recruit non-white officers especially in areas with minority communities.

The Scottish Government's 'Show Racism the Red Card' campaign, branded One Scotland, in which well-known footballers promote racial understanding aims to make people aware of the variety of cultures in modern Scotland, the amount of racism and what can be done about it.

Figure 3.12 →

Are the present laws successful?

Although many members of the Black and Asian communities are concentrated in the inner cities, where there are problems of poverty and social pressure/stress, progress has been made over the past 20 years in tackling racial disadvantage in Britain. Many individuals from a variety of ethnic minority groups have achieved success in their careers and in public life. The proportion of ethnic minority members who have professional and management positions jobs is also on the increase. There are at present 15 Black and Asian Members of Parliament, and the number of ethnic minority councillors in local government is growing (13 Labour MPs and 2 Conservative MPs). Black competitors have represented Britain in a range of sports (such as athletics, cricket and football) and ethnic minority talents in the arts and in entertainment have become more numerous.

Figure 3.13
Mohammed
Sarwar, MP →

However, many members of ethnic minorities would say that the law is not effective. They point to the fact that racist abuse still continues and that, on average, members of ethnic minorities have lower incomes than white Britons.

> 1   Why do some people say the present law is not effective enough?

> 1   Examine the success of measures to deal with inequalities related to ethnicity.

4 Inequalities in health

The National Health Service (NHS)

The NHS was set up in 1948 by a Labour Government as part of the Welfare State. Most British people still rely on the NHS for their healthcare. It is one of the most popular public services. However, it is now affected by problems and controversy especially over the ever increasing cost.

Why was the NHS set up?

Before the post 1945 Welfare State healthcare had been available to those who could pay. Those who could not afford to pay for a doctor went to hospitals which provided free clinics. This meant that health care was unequally distributed; better off areas had several doctors competing for custom. There was no integrated health plan for the country. Not enough was done to prevent ill health. However, improvements in public health as well as living standards meant that British people were in better health than in the past.

The original aims of NHS

- Universal – available throughout the country to everyone.
- Comprehensive – covering all aspects of health including prevention of disease.
- Integrated – hospitals, doctors and other services to co-operate in a planned way.
- Equal – everyone would be treated no matter what their personal circumstances were.
- Free at the point of use – no one would pay directly for their treatment as this would be covered by National Insurance.

> 1 What were the original aims of the NHS?

Early problems

It soon became obvious that the cost would be greater than planned for. It was expected that the first few years would be expensive as people were given treatment which they could not previously afford. However, the cost kept

Figure 4.1 →

going up. Within a few years prescription charges for medicine, glasses and dental treatment were introduced. National Insurance was not sufficient to cover the cost and the NHS has always had to be mainly (80%) paid for through general taxation.

> **1** Briefly describe the early problems of the NHS.

NHS achievements

People no longer worry about the cost of medical treatment. This means problems can be dealt with quickly before they get worse. Many new treatments and drugs have been developed. People live much longer.

> **1** What have been the main achievements of the NHS?

'A victim of its own success'

Healthcare is unlike most other industries. Most industries reduce their costs by replacing staff with new technology. This is important because wages are reasonably high in Britain and may be the biggest cost that the industry has. Health care is highly labour intensive – nearly 1 million people work for the NHS making it one of the biggest employers in Europe. Well over half of NHS expenditure is on staff. Many new developments actually need more staff. For example, a transplant operation might need twenty surgeons, nurses and technicians and take several hours. After the operation the patient will need total nursing care for weeks, sometimes months.

Although you frequently hear complaints that the NHS is under-funded, spending has increased every year. Health spending has doubled since 2000 and now takes around 9% of GDP. We no longer spend below the EU average

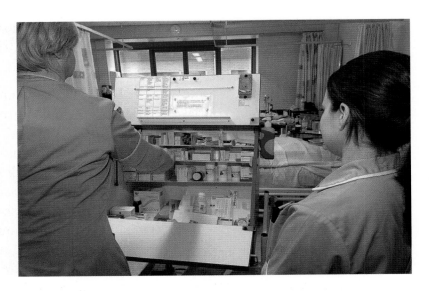

Figure 4.2 →

on health. In 2007–08, approximately £100 billion was allocated to the NHS – equivalent to over £1500 for each person in the country. Spending per person is higher in Scotland at around £2000 per head. This reflects the facts that Scotland has most of the remote areas in the UK and a poorer health record.

1 Explain in detail why the NHS is often described as a 'victim of its own success'?

2 What does most of the NHS budget get spent on?

3 How much does the NHS cost?

The NHS tries to meet its original aims of providing the best possible care for all patients. However, certain expensive drugs are not available to all patients. Some health authorities pay for some treatments, e.g. fertility, others do not. This is often referred to as a 'post code lottery'. There are some prescriptions drugs and medical procedures that may or may not be available depending on where you live. This is determined by the Health Board of that particular area approving specific prescription drugs or procedures. Prescription drugs can be very expensive (some are thousands of pounds per month) to provide on the NHS and it is believed that this is reason for them not being approved for use.

Figure 4.3 →

The fact that so many people now pay for private treatment, e.g. hip operations, shows the NHS is under pressure. Waiting lists are still a problem although they are now coming down.

The NHS cannot recruit enough doctors and nurses – in many areas it relies on foreign staff. Several countries, e.g. France, have more doctors/nurses per 1000 patients than the UK. As a response to this shortage, the NHS created NHS 24 to reduce the pressure on Accident and Emergency rooms, as well as GP services, particularly during the out of hours period. NHS is an online and telephone-based service available 24 hours a day. Users can access the service when they cannot get in touch with their own GP and are not well enough to wait. The website allows patients to answer 'yes' or 'no' questions about their condition in order to assess its severity. If they call the confidential phone number, they are directed to an appropriate health professional such as a nurse, pharmacist or dental nurse who will work with the user to address their concerns. NHS 24 was criticised in the past over the quality of advice given to callers, but serious problems arising from the service's use are few.

The NHS is not free at the point of need (use). Many pay prescription charges, also charges for optical/dental treatment. There is a crisis in the provision of dental treatment – in some areas it is now impossible to get dental treatment on the NHS. Dentists say NHS work is poorly paid – the government are now increasing the payments and have promised free NHS dental treatment for every child in Scotland who needs it.

1. What evidence is there of rationing in the NHS?
2. What other evidence is there to suggest that the NHS has been underfunded?
3. Is the NHS free at the point of use?
4. Explain the phrase 'post code lottery'.
5. Why has NHS24 been criticised?
6. Why is there concern over dental treatment?
7. Why has the cost of the Welfare State been higher than expected?

Some of the greatest health advances in the past were due to the introduction of clean water, proper sewage disposal, legal standards of food hygiene, as well as health initiatives such as vaccinations.

More money comes into the government in tax on alcohol etc. than is spent on public health campaigns. Drinks and tobacco companies aim advertising at young people, e.g. beer/lager brand names on football shirts (see figure 4.4 on page 72), Alcopops, Embassy Snooker.

1. To what extent has the NHS been able to meets its original aims.

Examine the outline written below. You can use it as a guide to write a complete 15 mark essay.

- **Introduction** – success of the NHS.
- **Paragraph 1** – universal but… shortage of dentists in some areas of Scotland, post code lottery.
- **Paragraph 2** – integrated but . . . often not enough cooperation between health boards and resources. Criticisms of NHS24.
- **Paragraph 3** – comprehensive – prevention of diseases largely successful but . . . difficult to change peoples' lifestyles, this would save NHS in the longer term.
- **Paragraph 4** – equal – mostly successful. Cannot limit service based on gender, race, sexuality or even lifestyle.
- **Paragraph 5** – free at the point of use. Funding of NHS. Originally with National Insurance, huge increase in cost than planned for. Increase in taxes? Introduction of some prescription charges?
- **In conclusion** – increasingly difficult to meet original aims largely due to 'infinite demand for finite resources'.

Figure 4.4 →

Evidence

Note that reasons and evidence overlap.

One of the original principles on which the NHS was based was equal access to health care. This has not been achieved. Life expectancy varies depending on where you live with Scotland being the lowest in the UK for both males and females from birth. There are also variations in life expectancy between cities and also even cities within the same region. Life expectancy at birth is at its highest level for both males and females. The three biggest causes of death in Scotland are cancers, coronary heart disease (CHD) and strokes.

Inequalities have increased in recent years. Certain groups within UK society have, on average, shorter lives and a greater chance of suffering health problems. Scotland, the north of England and Wales have poorer health records than south east England. These differences are linked to lifestyles with poorer health in former industrial areas. However, there are even greater differences within Scotland than between Scotland and south east England. This shows the real reason is not geography but poverty. As long ago as the early 1990s, the documentary 'Dead Poor' showed that on average people in middle class parts of Glasgow such as Bearsden live 10 years longer than in the working class Drumchapel council estate a few miles away. Babies born to poor mothers are twice as likely to die as those whose mothers are better off – this is linked to the mother's diet and whether she smoked during her pregnancy. Health inequalities actually increased in the UK during the 1980s and 1990s in line with the widening gap in living standards. League tables show that hospitals in cities with above average levels of poverty and unemployment – Glasgow, Liverpool and Manchester – are at the bottom of hospital league tables whereas those in well-off areas have the best records, e.g. Oxford which came out top.

1   What evidence is there of health inequalities in Britain today?
2   What has been happening to health inequalities?

The Black Report was published in 1980. It was the most thorough study ever made of the link between health and social class. It concluded that the general health of the population had improved but differences between rich and poor were widening whether by mortality (death rates) or morbidity (sickness rates which are harder to calculate). Black said that a child from a professional background was likely to live 5 years longer than a child from an unskilled, manual background. These inequalities start even before birth due to the different life styles of the parents.

Poor people are more likely to smoke, drink too much and eat poor diets. Their houses are more likely to suffer from damp and cold. The areas they live in have more accidents (e.g. high rise flats). Manual workers are more likely to be killed or injured at work. They are more likely to develop heart disease and several forms of cancer. Working class men are less likely to be aware of health issues and more likely to delay going to their doctor. Cultural factors make these men more likely to drink heavily than middle class males. Professional families can afford better diets and are more likely to encourage their children to eat what is good for them. Professional people (social classes A/B) are better educated, more aware of health issues, more likely to take exercise as well as having the money to join golf/fitness clubs. Owning a car makes it easier to get to shops with a good range of food and recreational opportunities etc.

Figure 4.5 →

1 What did the Black Report say?

2 Name the big three killer diseases in Scotland.

After the 1997 election, the New Labour Government asked a former Chief Medical Officer, **Sir Donald Acheson**, to set up a commission on inequalities in health. Acheson produced a report that said many of the same things the Black Report had. It said that in the UK there are still significant health differences between social classes and that the main cause of this is poverty.

Within Scotland, the gap between life expectancies for the poorest and the best off groups in society has widened and is now over 10 years. The better off are living longer and healthier lives but there has not been an improvement for the poorest groups. Those in the most deprived areas are over twice as likely to die from heart disease as those in affluent areas. Suicide rates are higher among poorer people, especially young men, and these have increased.

1 What were the findings of the Acheson report?

Health statistics based on postal districts or parliamentary constituencies all show striking differences between rich and poor areas.

It is estimated that one in four of all deaths in Scotland is from heart disease. There are three main causes of heart disease, these are unhealthy eating, lack of physical exercise and smoking. In 2000, Paisley was chosen by the then Scottish Executive to be one of four areas in Scotland to take part in a national health demonstration project. Paisley was chosen as it had one of the worst heart disease records in Scotland, with a great variation within the town of Paisley. The 'Have a Heart' project works with the people of Paisley to make better choices. It identifies people who are most at risk and those who have already been diagnosed with health problems. The project hopes to demonstrate to what degree health disease can be prevented. The 'Have a

Heart' project works with the local community to remove barriers to a healthier lifestyle and is part of the Heart Health Network, sharing its findings with other local areas.

Figure 4.6 Paisley town centre →

1 What is the purpose of the 'Have a Heart' project?

2 Is it a good idea for the government to help fund projects like this one? Why not?

3 Suggest some reasons why some people do not have healthy lifestyles.

There are also differences in health between males and females. Women live longer than men. Nowadays women rarely die in childbirth. From childhood, males are more likely to be injured or killed in accidents or other violent situations including fights and suicide. As they grow older men suffer more from heart disease and lung cancer. Although women live longer they suffer more ill health and are more likely to visit a doctor. Most women have children and this is one reason for this. Women are more likely to suffer respiratory problems and mental illness – perhaps due to stress. Women are more likely than men to be single parents or to look after elderly relatives. As women live longer than men and the elderly on average need twice as much medical attention than the rest of the population, it is not surprising that many more old ladies need health care than old men. Breast and cervical cancer are major causes of death among women. Other cancers are now increasing among women as they take up jobs that used to be done exclusively by men, which expose workers to chemicals, fumes and other hazards.

1 Make a summary of health differences between males and females.

There are some differences in health between ethnic minority groups and the rest of the UK population. Black people have lower rates of heart disease. However, Asians have even higher rates. Infant mortality is higher among minorities. This may be a result of language problems, poverty and reluctance

Figure 4.7 →

to go to the doctor. Some problems are limited to areas of origin. Asians are more likely to have Tuberculosis (TB). Blacks may carry sickle cell anaemia genes. Some of these differences are likely to disappear as an increasing percentage of minority groups are born in the UK.

Some argue that the private healthcare is evidence of inequality in that the better off can obtain treatment more quickly than others. Some procedures, e.g. IVF, and some expensive drugs are not always available under the NHS.

1   Summarise health issues that affect ethnic minorities.

2   To what extent do health inequalities still occur?

Reasons

Health inequalities are caused by a combination of poverty and lifestyle. Poorer people are less able to afford decent food, adequate housing, belong to health or sports clubs. They are more likely to be killed or injured at work, e.g. on building sites. They are less aware of health issues and less confident in talking to health professionals. They are more likely to suffer from financial concerns which can lead to stress and other health problems.

Poorer groups are more likely to have lifestyles which damage their health. Poor people are more likely to smoke, eat poor diets and take less exercise than those who are better off and better informed. Illegal drugs are a problem throughout the country but create greater problems in deprived areas.

These issues raise questions about the extent to which individuals should be responsible for living healthy lifestyles.

1   Give examples of the ways in which your lifestyle can affect your health.

Obesity is a growing problem in the UK. A recent report named Scotland as the most obese nation in the developed world behind the USA. Obesity can severely affect a person's quality of life, puts a strain on health services due to such medical conditions such as type 2 diabetes, hypertension and even premature death. The two major lifestyle factors associated with the growth of obesity are physical inactivity and poor diet.

Body Mass Index is the most commonly accepted measure of general obesity. BMI is calculated by dividing weight (measured in kilograms) by height squared (measured in metres). Adults are classed as overweight if their BMI is 25 or greater, obese if their BMI is 30 or more and morbidly obese if their BMI is 40 or more.

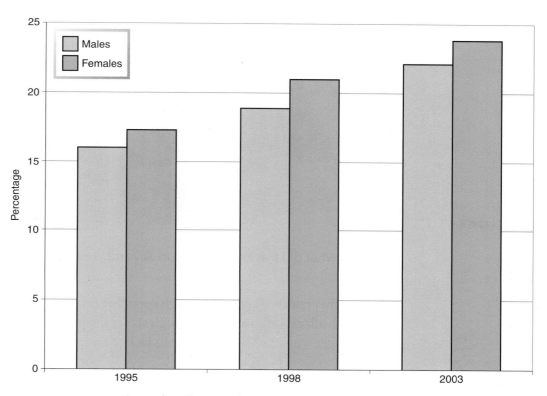

Figure 4.8 Levels of obesity in Scotland for adults aged 16–64 (1995-2003) →

Source: http://www.scotland.gov.uk/Topics/Statistics/Browse/Health/TrendObesity

The 2003 Scottish Health Survey estimated that in Scotland around 22% of men and 24% of women were obese. These figures show a marked increase in obesity levels since 1995 when 16% of men and 17% of women were obese. Perhaps more worrying is that 64% of Scottish men and more than half of women (57%) were overweight (including obese) in 2003.

1 What does it mean to be obese?

2 What problems can obesity lead to for individuals and for the government?

3 Explain why the BMI may not be the best way to determine obesity levels.

Responses

First Black and then Acheson recommended large-scale improvements not just in NHS spending but on more housing for rent, pensions and DWP benefits, free healthy food in schools and subsidies to cut the cost of fruit and vegetables to give poorer people in the UK the chance to live healthier and longer lives. Acheson also wants more done to discourage young people from taking up smoking through a big tax increase on cigarettes to make them prohibitively expensive, a total ban on advertising of tobacco, free nicotine patches etc. to get more adults to give up. The report also recommended tougher controls over the promotion of 'junk'-type foods which are often too high in salt or sugar.

Figure 4.9 →

1   What did the Acheson Report say and recommend?

Another concern was not enough spending on other public services, e.g. housing which affect health and not enough screening programmes, e.g. for breast cancer in younger women. There is a serious lack of awareness of health issues among men.

These were introduced in the early days of the NHS in response to the rising costs of drugs. Many people are exempt. Recently, the Scottish Government has announced its intention to phase out charges in Scotland. They have already been abolished in Wales. The UK government intends to keep prescription charges in England. They argue that those who can afford to contribute to the NHS should do so and that poor people, the elderly and children do not pay. The Scottish Government argue that free prescriptions mean a return to the original principles of the NHS, free at the point of need.

1   What are the government's plans for prescription charges in Scotland?

Health care is devolved. This means that the Scottish Government and the UK Government are both responsible for doing something about health inequalities. Some measures specifically target poor groups while others apply to everyone but deal with conditions that most affect the poor.

1 Explain the significance of health in Scotland being a devolved issue.

Note that new initiatives on health appear frequently. It is impossible to remember them all! Here are a few recent ones:

- Targets and incentives for GPs in certain areas such as the Deprived Practice Allowance.
- National Targets, e.g. reduction in heart disease, cancers.
- Recent bans on smoking in public have been introduced in Scotland in 2006 and extended to England in 2007.
- Raising the age to buy cigarettes to 18 years.

Figure 4.10 →

- Community Health Partnerships.
- Multi-agency approaches where health, education, housing, social work and police work together in deprived areas.
- Plans to increase PE in and out of schools.
- The Disability Equality Duty requires all public authorities to ensure that all disabled people are treated fairly.
- 2008 Scottish GPs agreed to work evening and weekend hours.
- The Hungry for Success initiative.
- Closing the Opportunity Gap (More Choice, More Chances).

- Health promotions in specific local councils providing breakfast clubs, fruit in schools, chilled water, Fuel Zone Points Reward Project where pupils collect points for making healthy food choices. Points can be later redeemed for cinema tickets, video games etc.
- Clearer food packaging to indicate levels of fat and salt – a traffic light system is often used by many food manufacturers.

Figures 4.11 and 4.12 →

1   What is happening to the overall health of British people?

2   Choose two measures that have been taken recently to improve public health and evaluate whether you think they are a good idea or not.

3   Select one government response that you think is effective in reducing inequalities.

Health, work and well-being strategy

This is an example of a multi-agency approach. The government aims to improve the general health and well-being of the working age population. This will in turn reduce the number of people taking sick leave and claiming sickness benefits. Working together with employers, trade unions and healthcare professionals, they hope to create healthier workplaces, ensure provision of good occupational health services and enhance rehabilitation support.

The 'health, work and well-being strategy' is a partnership between the Department of Health, the DWP, the Health and Safety Executive, the Welsh Assembly Government and the Scottish Government. By working together, it is hoped that more people are able to work, they are happy and healthy at work, and that those with health problems or disabilities can benefit from improved working opportunities.

Task visit: www.healthyliving.gov.uk to find out more information on healthy lifestyles and what initiatives the government wants to promote to the public.

Are the measures working?

Many of the government's health initiatives have had limited success. The NHS is busier and more expensive to run than ever. More drugs and treatments are available to patients, but at an ever increasing cost to the taxpayer. However, the overall health of British people is better than ever. Life expectancy continues to increase. However, differences between groups within society have increased. As the better off and better educated live longer and healthier lives the health gaps between them and the poorest groups has widened. Some groups have not seen any improvement in their health and this is linked to lifestyle which in turn is linked to poverty and social exclusion.

The discussion over the role of the government and health inequalities comes back to the debate over individual or collective responsibilities. Should people be able to eat what they want, even if it is bad for their health? Should the NHS treat people who have brought poor health on themselves due to poor lifestyle choices?

5 The SQA exam

Paper One

You will have to do one 15 mark question from a choice of two in Section B in around 22 minutes.

You must answer the question on the exam paper and not what you hoped the question would be! This means taking a moment to think what is required. Remember you will not be able to use all your knowledge in 22 minutes. All Paper One questions expect you to evaluate and to reach a balanced conclusion.

You should apply the following procedure:

● Make a point – give an example – make a comment – then move on.
● Key words such as **however**, **although**, **on the other hand** indicate that you are discussing and not just describing.
● Start with a strong opening statement that shows the marker you understand the question. Your opening statement will lead into a series of paragraphs and to a balanced conclusion.
● A balanced conclusion is not the same as a summary.

These points are demonstrated in the following specimen answers.

Q 'Policies to reduce inequalities in health in the UK have been largely unsuccessful'.
Discuss.

15

Specimen Answer 1

Health inequalities in the UK have widened in recent years. The health of the better off and better educated has improved but that of the poorest groups in society has not. This is linked to lifestyles and life chances. Poorer people are still more likely to smoke, eat poor diets, drink excessively, live in sub-standard housing and suffer from stress or be injured at work.

Links between poverty and health were shown in the Black Report and more recently by Acheson and other surveys which concluded that the situation had not improved and that health inequalities could not be solved by the NHS alone.

Recent governments have set targets to reduce heart disease, cancers, infant mortality and other diseases linked to lifestyle. However, many targets have not been met. The NHS has had a big increase in funding; however, much of this has gone on salaries and replacing out-of-date buildings. More recent health policy aims to put more resources into primary care and give extra help in deprived areas and concentrate on mothers and young children.

Health care is devolved. Scottish health policy has similar targets to the rest of the UK. However, spending per person is higher in Scotland, at around £2000 per person, which the Scottish Government say is needed as we have higher levels of deprivation. Scotland introduced a public smoking ban ahead of England and there has already been an improvement in public health.

Attempts to improve diet have had limited success. Schools now have healthy eating policies but the well-publicised Jamie Oliver campaign has led to fewer children in England taking school lunches.

There is a shortage of affordable housing which can lead to health problems due to damp buildings or stress.

Although unemployment is now low many people feel forced into jobs they dislike and work-related stress has increased. However, health and safety rules have reduced accidents in work places.

Some minority groups have special health problems e.g. sickle cell anaemia. Information in a range of languages is now available. Men's health has been targeted as men are less likely to consult doctors. However, working class men still have poorer health than professionals.

Campaigns to persuade the public to live healthy lifestyles have been more effective with the better off. Some say the government should do more to control the advertising and promotion of junk food and alcohol. Governments receive large sums from tax on cigarettes and alcohol which could be hypothecated to the NHS and other priorities, e.g. low-cost housing.

In conclusion, the many improvements in healthcare have not reduced health inequalities which will not disappear without tougher government action as well as lifestyle changes throughout society.

Q **Examine the effectiveness of responses to inequalities in income in the UK.** `15`

Specimen Answer 2

The post-war welfare state aimed to provide a basic standard of living for all UK citizens through a system of National Insurances. Benefits reflected the collectivist approach as several were universal. However, means testing was used for some selective benefits.

Although living standards have improved throughout the UK differences in income and wealth have widened. Poverty still exists although it is relative rather than absolute. Recent governments, both Conservative and New Labour, have emphasised individual responsibility through the policy that help from the state should increasingly be based on means tested benefits.

Social security benefits are still the main way in which the government supports those on low incomes. However, social security benefits have been reformed as part of the Welfare to Work policy which the government say is needed to reduce social exclusion.

The New Deal encourages claimants off benefits into work by providing training, improved childcare and other incentives. Unemployment Benefit is now Jobs Seekers Allowance and becomes means tested after 6 months. Incapacity Benefit is being changed to reduce the numbers not working due to disability. Tax Credits give selective help to groups such as families; single parent families have the highest poverty rates.

These changes have had some success. Child poverty has been reduced but not eliminated as nearly one-quarter of children in Scotland live poverty. Fewer people are unemployed although this is due to the world economy and some people claim they are forced into unsuitable jobs. However, there is a shortage of affordable housing, mortgage repossessions are at record levels and consumer debt is at an all time high.

Women still on average earn lower incomes than men despite Equal Opportunities legislation. However, some claim the glass ceiling is now cracked as girls outperform boys throughout education and are now increasingly succeeding in the workplace. New requirements for all public bodies to guarantee equal opportunities should make a big difference. The new Commission for Equality and Human Rights (CEHR) has been set up to ensure equality throughout the UK. Although racism and discrimination still occur, some ethnic minorities such as Chinese and Indians now do as well as the white majority.

In conclusion, inequalities in income will continue. They are inevitable in a free-market society. However, it is essential that help is provided for the unsuccessful as society suffers if an underclass exist which is socially excluded and a source of crime and anti-social behaviour.

 To what extent do inequalities in ethnicity and gender continue to exist? | 15 |

Specimen Answer 3

Introduction – Women's traditional role made it difficult for them to progress socially and economically. Ethnic minorities often experience direct and indirect discrimination.

You should write several paragraphs in which you make reference to:

- Evidence – jobs, education
- Reasons – discrimination, direct and indirect discrimination
- Responses – legislation, old and new, gender equality duty (GED), CEHR, 'glass ceiling'.

In conclusion, inequalities in ethnicity and gender are still present in the UK despite attempts over many years to improve the situation. However, there is also evidence of improvement for some women and minority group members. Recent legislation should further improve the situation.

Quick Revision Test Questions

Test your knowledge of this topic by honestly asking yourself if you can answer these 25 questions.

1. What were the principles of the Welfare State?
2. What were the original aims of the NHS?
3. How was the Welfare State to be paid for?
4. Why has cost been such a problem?
5. Explain the term 'social safety net'.
6. What has happened to living standards in the UK?
7. What has happened to differences between rich and poor?
8. What is meant by relative poverty?
9. What problems can social exclusion lead to?
10. Name the main groups of benefits and give an example of each.
11. What are the advantages of selective benefits?
12. What are two problems with selective benefits?
13. What is the difference between collectivism and individualism?
14. Give examples of declining and expanding inequalities.
15. Can you explain New Deal, Tax Credits, Welfare to Work?
16. What does the CEHR do?
17. What is the 'glass ceiling'?
18. Are women now equal to men?
19. What is the difference between indirect and direct discrimination?
20. Describe recent changes to immigration policy.
21. Describe recent attempts to end discrimination.
22. Why do some say welfare reform is essential?
23. Name the three biggest causes of death in Scotland.
24. Give three pieces of evidence for health inequalities.
25. Describe recent proposals to reduce health inequalities?

The Decision Making Exercise (DME)

A Decision Making Exercise on Health & Wealth – 30 marks in 1 hour 15 minutes.

There are three or four short Evaluating questions together worth 10 marks which you will do first. These are designed to make you familiar with the material for the 20 mark Report – all the answers are in the Sources – just like Standard Grade. Provided you are careful and quote the correct sources they should give you a good mark out of 10 to set you up for the big report you have to write in Question 4.

Do not spend too long on these short questions – use the marks available as a guide, each is worth 2 or 3 marks – spend no longer than 25 minutes on them. Two mark questions usually ask you to contrast two views or identify an incorrect/exaggerated statement. Three mark questions often start with 'To what extent' and involve a statement(s) that is/are part right part wrong.

For Question 4 – the 20 mark report – you will be given written and statistical sources on a current social issue and asked to recommend one of two courses of action. Do not worry if the issue is unfamiliar. All the detail you need is in the question paper. You do need to bring in general background knowledge of inequalities. The work you have done for Paper One Section B will cover this.

First make your decision. Then mark up the question paper with a list of reasons **for** and **against** your decision.

Start the report:

Chapter 1 – Introduction, Role and Remit

This is where you clearly state your recommendation.

Chapter 2 – Then a much longer chapter giving reasons for your recommendation, backed up by statistics and other evidence from the Sources (quote them all) and using sub headings. You will base your recommendation on one of the major written sources. You will probably find less time pressure in Paper 2 than in Paper 1 so make sure you use all the source material and write as much as you can. Make sure you integrate the written and statistical Sources, e.g. Source A says that...and this is backed up by Source C3 which shows that...

Annotate the margins whenever you use a source – A, B, C1, C2, C3 or Background Knowledge (BK).

You must bring in some background knowledge – make sure it is also integrated with other material, e.g. Source C2 shows that death rates are linked to poverty: this was also shown in a recent documentary on different parts of Glasgow.

Examples of background knowledge could be:

- A local issue.
- Recent newspapers/TV stories.
- Whether a proposal does/does not meet the original aims of the Welfare State – a safety net from the 'cradle to the grave'.
- The conflict caused by infinite demand for limited resources – the Welfare State is a victim of its own success – early expectations that the cost would level off have been wrong and it needs more every year, e.g. NHS.
- Governments have been criticised for not spending enough yet NHS spending has gone up every year.
- Recent governments have all promised to hold down Income Tax making it difficult to put more into the Welfare State but rises in National Insurance means the NHS is now catching up with the EU average.
- You could even bring in your own or your family's personal experience.
- Differences between Scotland and England.
- Increased role of private sector.

Chapter 3 – a chapter saying why you did not choose the other option (Rebuttal) with details of problems and cost implications.

Chapter 4 – Summary and Conclusion
Finish with a short Summary and Conclusion in which you repeat your recommendation with a very brief summary of your main arguments.

You can use more subheadings but you must not write the report as an essay. You must use all the sources but not necessarily in every chapter.

Then go over everything to make sure you have used all the Sources and brought in background knowledge, integrated them all and not contradicted yourself.

The following outline shows how to go about this.

> ### Chapter 1 – Introduction, Role and Remit
>
> *I am an expert in social policy. I have been asked to recommend whether Child Benefit should be means tested or continue as a universal benefit and given to all families. I recommend that it should remain a universal benefit.*
>
> ### Chapter 2 – Reasons to support my recommendation
>
> **A**   *I agree with the pressure group spokesperson when they say that this benefit is an*
>
> **BK** *essential part of the modern Welfare State. The collectivist principles of the Beveridge*
>
> **C1** *era are still relevant today. Source C1 shows that families with children are the group*
>
> **A**   *most affected by poverty throughout the UK. In Source A, the spokesperson is right to point out that the great majority of families need some assistance with the cost of bringing up children.*
>
> ### Chapter 3 – Rebuttal: why I rejected the other option
>
> **B**   *In Source B, the economist claims that the UK can no longer afford universal benefits.*
>
> **C2b** *However, Source C2b shows that the UK is a wealthy country which spends less on its children than many of its western European neighbours. The economist is also wrong*
>
> **B**   *to say that means testing is a fair system. The take up rate of means tested benefits is*
>
> **BK** *low which means that many citizens are living in hardship.*
>
> ### Chapter 4 – Summary and Conclusion
>
> *I have recommended that Child Benefit should continue to be paid universally and not means tested. My main reasons are:*
>
> - *The original principles of the Welfare State are still relevant today.*
> - *Means testing leads to lower take up, hardship and an increase in social exclusion.*
> - *Families are under increasing pressure and need assistance from the State.*
> - *Comparisons with other developed countries show that the UK needs to maintain a decent level of support for families with children.*
> - *Means tested benefits should be used to top up Child Benefit where appropriate but not to replace it.*

Index

2001 Census
   ethnic groups 54, 56

Acheson Report 74, 78
adults
   working age 1
advertising 71
affluent areas 11
Afro-Caribbean community 55, 57
alcohol advertising 71
apprenticeships 25
Asian British 55–6, 67, 75–6
asylum seekers 60, 61
Attendance Allowance 28–9

Bangladeshi community 56
benefits
   asylum seekers 61
   cost 3, 27, 30
   incapacity 33
   income 6–7
   recipients 27
   Social Security 26–30
Bereavement Allowance 29
Beveridge Report 2–3
Black British 55, 57, 67, 75–6
Black Report 73–4, 78
blue collar workers 36
body mass index (BMI) 77
Britain
   citizenship 61
   life expectancy 1, 73
   population 1
   see also England
Business Link 25

cancer 75

car ownership 7, 8
Carer's Allowance 29
Carer's Credit 50
Child Benefit 28
child care 34, 50, 52
child poverty 16–18, 19, 21
   government targets 34
   reduction 31, 35
Child Poverty Action Group (CPAG) 13, 35
Child Poverty Unit 34
Child Support Agency (CSA) 32
Child Tax Credit 29
Chinese community 56
cigarette spending 11
citizenship 61
cohabitation 42
Cold Weather Payment 29
collectivism 4
Commission for Racial Equality (CRE) 66
Commonwealth
   migration to Britain 55
Community Care 19
computer ownership 9
consumer goods 7, 8–9
contributory benefits 26
convenience foods 7
council housing 20
Council Tax Benefit 28
couple families
   poverty 14, 15
CPAG see Child Poverty Action Group
CRE see Commission for Racial Equality
crime 39

Crime and Disorder Act 1998 66
CSA see Child Support Agency

decision making exercise (DME) 87
dental treatment 71
diet 7, 77, 78, 80
digital television ownership 9
direct discrimination 47
disability benefits 26
Disability Equality Duty 79
discrimination
   forms 47–8
   legislation 65–6
   racial 64, 67
disposable income 13
divorce 42
DME see decision making exercise
domestic violence 51
drugs
   illegal use 76
   treatment cost 70
DWP see Social Security benefits

earnings
   men 44
   women 43, 44
eating habits 7, 77, 78, 80
economic development 25
education
   poverty 21
   social class 38
   women 46
Education Maintenance Allowance (EMA) 32–3

EHRC *see* Equality and Human Rights Commission
elderly
    health 75
    illness 20
    income 15
    population 1
    poverty 17, 19, 43
    Social Security benefits 27
EMA *see* Education Maintenance Allowance
employment 21–6
    educational qualifications 47
    gender 47
    regional differences 12, 21–2
    sex discrimination 47–8, 49, 51
    social class 36–8
    see also work
Employment Protection Act 48
Employment and Support Allowance (ESA) 30, 33
England
    unemployment 22
    see also Britain
equal opportunities 48–51
    ethnic minorities 65
    public service agreements 66
Equal Pay Act 1970 48
Equality and Human Rights Commission (EHRC) 48–9, 66
ESA *see* Employment and Support Allowance
ethnic groups
    composition 54, 56
    home ownership 63–4
    poverty 62
    unemployment 62–3
ethnic minorities
    achievements 67
    distribution 55
    health 75–6

income 15
    inequalities 54–67
    Members of Parliament 67
    population 56
    poverty 15
    racism 64, 67
    support 65
    work 67
European Convention against Human Trafficking 51
European Union (EU)
    member countries 58
    migration to UK 57, 58
exam paper samples 82–9

families
    average 8
    poverty 15
    traditional roles 45
    types 41
Family Credit *see* Working Tax Credit
flexible working 25
food labelling 80
foreign holidays 7
foreign workers 54, 58–9, 60
free prescriptions 78
free school meals 26
Fuel Poverty 20

GDP (gross domestic product) 6
gender
    inequalities 40–53
    pay gap 42–3
Gender Equality Duty (GED) 49
Glasgow
    child poverty 16
    life expectancy 20
GNP (gross national product) 6
government initiatives
    health 79–81
    welfare reform 30–5

gross domestic product (GDP) 6
gross national product (GNP) 6

'Have a Heart' project 74–5
health 68–81
    government initiatives 79–81
    lifestyle 73–5, 76, 78, 81
    poverty 21
    regional differences 73
    social class 38, 73–4
    spending 69–70
Health Boards 70
heart disease 74
holidays 7
home ownership 8, 9
    ethnic groups 63–4
home repossessions 19
households
    activities 43
    poverty 15, 16–17
    size 1
    types 40, 41
housing
    damp 20
    social class 38
Housing Benefit 26, 28
housing estates 39
human trafficking 51

immigration 54, 57–61
    benefits/cost 58
    restrictions 57, 58–9
    source countries 60
incapacity benefits 33
income
    average family 8
    definition 6
    inequalities 6–39
    social class 38
Income Support (IS) 26, 28
Income Tax 22–3
Indian community 55–6
indirect discrimination 48

individualism 4
inequality
    ethnicity 54–67
    gender 40–53
    health 68–81
    solutions 35
infant mortality 75
internet access 8, 9
IS *see* Income Support

job sharing 25
Jobcentre plus 25
jobs *see* employment; work
Jobseeker's Allowance (JSA) 22,
    28
Joseph Rowntree Foundation 14
junk food 78

legislation
    racism 65–6
leisure activities
    poverty 21
life expectancy 1, 20, 73
lifestyle
    health 73–5, 76, 78, 81
living standards
    improvement 7
    inequalities 6–39
    regional differences 10
London
    child poverty 16, 18
lone parents *see* single parent
    families
low pay 19, 20, 23, 43

manual work 36
marriage 41
married couples
    number 8
means-tested benefits 7, 19, 26,
    27, 28
men
    earnings 44

health 75
life expectancy 1
pension age 33
traditional roles 45–7
work 45
middle class 36, 37–8
    health 73–4
    traditional roles 45
migrant workers 54, 58–9, 60
mobile phone ownership 9

National Health Service (NHS)
    68–81
    achievements 69
    aims 68
    cost 3
    expenditure 69–70
    NHS 24 70–1
    problems 68–9
National Insurance 3, 26, 69
National Minimum Wage
    (NMW) 31–2, 51
naturalisation 61
New Deal 26–30, 31, 51
New Labour
    welfare reform 30
NHS 24 70–1
    see also National Health
        Service
NMW *see* National Minimum
    Wage
non-contributory benefits 26
North-South Divide 10

obesity 77
occupational groups
    earnings 44
occupational pensions 7
One Scotland 66
out of work benefits 18, 20, 26, 28

Paisley (Scotland)
    project 74–5

Pakistani community 56
Parliament
    ethnic minorities 67
    women 51, 53
part-time work 23, 25, 46
Paternity Leave and Pay 50
pay bonuses 22
pay gap 42–3
PBS *see* points-based
    immigration system
Pension Credit 29, 50
pensioner poverty 17, 43
    see also elderly
pensions 7, 29, 33
personal wealth 9
pet ownership 8
points-based immigration
    system (PBS) 58–9
police 66
political parties
    social class 36–9
poor areas 11
population 1, 56
poverty 13–19
    definition 13
    ethnic groups 62
    health 73, 76, 81
    line 14–16
    social exclusion 24
Poverty and Social Exclusion
    Survey (PSE) 14
prescription charges 69, 71, 78
private healthcare 71, 76
professions *see* employment;
    work
programme centres 25
public service agreements 66

Race Relations Act 1976 65
Race Relations (Amendment)
    Act 2000 66
racism 64, 65–6, 67
ready meals 7

refugees 60, 61
relative poverty 13
repossessions (homes) 19
retirement
    age 52
    income 7
    pension 29, 33
revision questions 86
rich areas 11

safety net benefits 19
SAQ exam papers 82–9
satellite/cable digital TV 9
school health promotions 80
Scotland
    child poverty 16, 18, 34
    earnings 44
    employment 21–2
    health 70, 73, 74, 77
    life expectancy 73
    obesity 77
    population 1
    poverty 15, 16, 18, 20, 34
    racism 66
    unemployment 10
    women in Parliament 53
Scottish Enterprise 25
Scottish Index of Multiple
    Deprivation 14
screening programmes 78
selective benefits 27, 28
senior citizens see elderly
separation 42
sex discrimination 47–8, 49, 51
Sex Discrimination Act 1975
    48
share ownership 9
sickle cell anaemia 76
single parent families
    New Deal 51
    poverty 14, 15, 16, 17, 19
    women 42
skills shortages 59

smoking 78
    bans 12, 79
    children 12
    cost 11
SMP see Statutory Maternity
    Pay
social class 35–9
    definitions 36–7
    health 38, 73–4
social exclusion 24
Social Fund 29
Social Security benefits 26–30
spending
    affluent/poor 10
    cigarettes 11
    couples/families 8
    government 24
    health 69–70
    regional differences 11
Standard Occupational
    Classification 37
state pension 29, 33
Statutory Maternity Pay (SMP)
    49
students 32–3
suicide 74
Sure Start 32

tax credits 19, 31, 34
taxes
    personal income 6
television ownership 9
trafficking 51
training schemes 25
Training for Work 25
tuberculosis (TB) 76

underclass 24, 38–9
unemployment 21–6
    benefits 20, 26, 28
    child poverty 18, 19
    ethnic groups 62–3
    levels 3, 10

poverty 15, 19
    regional differences 12, 21–2
    UK 22, 23
universal benefits 26, 28

waiting lists 71
wealth 6–39
    definition 6
    personal 9
wealthy areas 11
welfare
    government initiatives 30–5
    provision 4
    state 2–5
well-being strategy 80
white collar workers 36
Winter Fuel Payment 29
women
    children 40–1, 42
    earnings 43, 44
    education 46
    health 75
    income 14, 20
    life expectancy 1
    Members of Parliament 51,
        53
    part-time work 46
    social class 37
    state pension 33, 43
    traditional roles 45–7
    work 42–3, 45, 49, 52
work
    ethnic minorities 67
    gender differences 45
    health 80
    stress 23
    women 42–3, 45, 49, 52
    see also employment
working class 36, 37–8
    health 73
    traditional roles 45
working population 8
Working Tax Credit 29, 50